THE UNLIKELY HERO

1

Chronicles of *the* Yellowstone Wolves

★

RICK McINTYRE AND DAVID A. POULSEN

THE
UNLIKELY
HERO

The Story of Wolf 8

GREYSTONE KIDS
GREYSTONE BOOKS • VANCOUVER/BERKELEY/LONDON

Greystone Kids / Greystone Books Ltd.
greystonebooks.com

Cataloguing data available from Library and Archives Canada
ISBN 978-1-77840-022-3 (cloth)
ISBN 978-1-77840-023-0 (epub)

Editing by Linda Pruessen
Copy editing by Dawn Loewen
Proofreading by Alison Strobel
Cover and interior design by Jessica Sullivan
Cover illustration by Lieke van der Vorst
Interior illustrations by John Potter

Printed and bound in Canada on FSC®-certified paper at Friesens. The FSC® label
means that materials used for the product have been responsibly sourced.

This book was written after Rick McIntyre finished working for the
National Park Service. Nothing in the writing is intended or should be
interpreted as expressing or representing the official policy or positions
of the U.S. government or any government departments or agencies.

Greystone Books thanks the Canada Council for the Arts, the British Columbia Arts
Council, the Province of British Columbia through the Book Publishing Tax Credit,
and the Government of Canada for supporting our publishing activities.

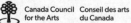

MIX
Paper from
responsible sources
FSC® C102842

BRITISH COLUMBIA

BRITISH COLUMBIA
ARTS COUNCIL
An agency of the Province of British Columbia

Canada Council   Conseil des arts
for the Arts   du Canada

Greystone Books gratefully acknowledges the xʷməθkʷəy̓əm (Musqueam),
Sḵwx̱wú7mesh (Squamish), and səl̓ilwətaɬ (Tsleil-Waututh) peoples on
whose land our Vancouver head office is located.

*To the memory of my mom, who
passed away during the writing of this book.
Though she never got to see or read it,
I know she would have been proud of it,
as she was of all of my books. Love you, Mom.*

DAVID

Contents

A Note About This Book

No one knows exactly what a wolf thinks. But after decades of watching their behavior, the people who study these amazing animals can imagine what is going on in a wolf's mind. Like their cousins, the domesticated dogs, wolves will often let us know what they are feeling and thinking through body language and sounds. This book looks at the life of Wolf 8, a famous wolf that was part of the reintroduction program that brought wolves back to Yellowstone National Park in 1995. Wolf 8's life was observed most closely by biologist and wolf expert Rick McIntyre. No one knew 8 better and no one is better able to convey what he might have been thinking at any given time. It is Rick's years of observations, of watching and studying Wolf 8 and the other Yellowstone wolves, that are at the heart of this book.

Rick and other wolf biologists witnessed many of the events you'll read about here—and in sidebars throughout Wolf 8's story, you'll hear directly from Rick about his work. Descriptions of other incidents that were not witnessed are based on sightings of wolves in similar situations. ★ DAVID

The Wolf Pup

The wolf pup sniffed the winter air and looked around. A cold wind swirled in the nearby trees. The pines that were everywhere bent as if to escape the bitter gusts. Clouds hung low in the sky; the sun would make no appearance on this day.

The wolf pup didn't move. He was scared. In fact, he'd been scared for a long time now and didn't really understand what was happening to him. This was a new place, a different place. But the wolf pup didn't know that or care. He was wishing he could be back where he'd been before, where he had always been.

Some days earlier, the young wolf and his family—his father, mother, and three brothers—had been captured by humans and placed in separate cages. He was the smallest of the four pups in the family and the last one to be captured. In fact, he'd almost been left behind when the human captors hadn't seen him right away.

The cages were placed inside a container that was nothing like anything the wolf pup and his family had ever experienced. It felt like a cave, but one that the wolves could not walk out of whenever they wanted to. The container and the cages it carried, each with a wolf inside, soon began to move. It had seemed to the wolf pup that the moving and bouncing went on for a very long time. The endless motion made the wolf pup's stomach feel queasy, and a few times he threw up.

The wolves were being transported in a horse trailer from Alberta, Canada, where they had been captured, to Yellowstone National Park in the American state of Wyoming. The wolf pup hadn't liked the long journey. The clatter of the cages jostling and bumping into one another and the unpleasant feeling of the trailer's movement made the journey seem endless. For a time, as the convoy of trailers moved through southern Alberta, it seemed to the pup that it was getting warmer around him. And it was. An Alberta chinook wind brought warm air out of the west, but then, as the trailers moved farther south into Montana, it grew colder again. There were scary roaring noises outside the big container too, first coming closer and getting louder and louder, and then fading away. In the woods where he had spent his early life, the wolf pup had never seen or heard huge highway trucks, so he was unfamiliar with the noise they made as they thundered by. Each time, the noise frightened him. He got down on his belly when the loud noise came closer and grew louder, and did not get back up on his feet until the noise had faded away.

With each wolf in its own cage, the pup was apart from his mother, father, and brothers. To the wolf pup, the container was closed in and dark, something like the den he had known when he was very young. But in this much bigger den he couldn't get close to the other members of his family. Even though they were nearby and he could smell them, he couldn't press up against his mother or playfully nip at his father. The wolf pup was hungry and he was tired. He'd tried sleeping, but except for a few short naps, that had been almost impossible. He wished that all of this would end, and that he could get back to the world and the life he was used to.

And then, all at once, it did end. The moving and bouncing stopped. The pup felt a lot better when he was finally let out of his cage and allowed to join his family. They were together again, and that part was good, but they were in a strange place, a place he had never been before. It looked different, it smelled different... all of it *was* different. The feel of the coarse grass where it poked through the snow, the bushes, even the trees— none of it was the same. The low clouds made this new place feel somehow smaller, and not at all friendly.

As he looked at this new world around him, he was confused—and frightened. The wolf pup looked at his brothers. Though they were bigger, they appeared to be as worried and nervous as he was.

He moved closer to his mother, hoping that she would somehow let him know that whatever was happening to them was okay, that he didn't need to be afraid. But although she didn't show any of the fear he was feeling, the pup sensed that all of this was new to her too. In fact, both his mother and his father seemed nervous and unsure.

There were things the wolf pup didn't know, things he *couldn't* know. He didn't know, for example, that he and his family were part of something called the Yellowstone Wolf Reintroduction Project. He didn't know that they were among fourteen wolves—three families (or packs) and one lone male—that had been captured in Canada to be moved to the United States.

The six wolves that made up the pup's family were not released into the wild, at least not right away. Instead, they had been placed in an acclimation pen, a large, fenced enclosure that allowed no possibility of escape. This was partly because wolves have a homing instinct, and if they'd simply been turned loose they would have headed north, back toward Canada. But the pen was also there to keep them safe: they wouldn't have to face the dangers and challenges of their new surroundings right away.

The wolf pup also didn't know that for almost seventy years there had been no wolves in Yellowstone National Park. The last wolves in the park had been shot and killed in 1926 by park rangers, at a time when humans didn't understand or trust wolves and wanted them gone. And from that time until now, in 1995, in this part of the world they had been gone.

But in recent years the National Park Service realized that eliminating the wolves had been a terrible mistake. Wolves had been a part of this land for thousands of years before Yellowstone National Park even existed. Their carefully planned extinction from their homeland was more than unfortunate—it was tragic. And now government decision-makers wanted to right that wrong. With the reintroduction plan, that was happening.

Not everyone was happy to see the wolves return. There were those who would stop at nothing to get rid of the new arrivals. Ranchers who lived near Yellowstone were worried that the wolves would range outside the park's boundaries and attack their livestock. In fact, there had been death threats made against the wolves. Because of those threats, park rangers guarded and protected the packs during the ten weeks they were in their acclimation enclosures. Those rangers patrolled around the clock, often in deep snow and freezing conditions, to ensure that no harm came to the newcomers. And none did.

But maybe the most important thing the wolf pup didn't know was that he now had a name. To the people who had captured him and to those who would watch and study him in his new home, he was known as Wolf 8. His father was Wolf 4, his mother Wolf 5, and his three brothers Wolves 2, 3, and 6. Because they had been released near Yellowstone's Crystal Creek, they were designated the Crystal Creek pack.

Wolf 8 and his brothers had been born eight months before their long journey from Alberta to Wyoming. Except for their age, there wasn't much about them that was the same. 8's three siblings had shiny black coats, like their father. And also like their father, who was the biggest wolf that Wolf 8 had ever seen, his brothers were tall and husky. 8's fur was a drab shade of gray, while his mother had a beautiful whitish coat. And he was smaller than his brothers, the runt of the litter.

8 had discovered early on that being the smallest wasn't a good thing. For the first few weeks after the pups had been born, the rough-and-tumble play between them was fun. But as they grew older, 8's siblings also became rougher. The three of them chased him around the pen and bullied him. And, three against one, they ganged up on him when they were playfighting, often pinning him to the ground and biting him. Wolf bites, even from young wolves, hurt. 8 was constantly watching his brothers, wondering when the next attack would happen. It might come when he was eating, or even when he was sleeping. With his dull gray fur standing out in sharp contrast to the sleek black coats

of his larger siblings, 8 often stayed a little way off from the rest of his family, hoping to avoid his brothers. But still the bullying continued. Sometimes after his brothers had beaten up on him, his mother would gently lick 8 on the face and in the places where he had been bitten. That always made him feel better.

The days in the acclimation enclosure passed slowly. Because they were in a confined space, the wolf family couldn't go hunting for food the way they had when they lived in Canada. Instead, the biologists came by twice a week to drop off elk, deer, and bison carcasses for the wolves to feed on. 8 was usually the last to eat. His brothers saw to that.

More than any of the family, 8 longed to wander, to travel farther than the acclimation pen allowed. He quickly grew tired of seeing the same trees, the same snowdrifts piled high against the deadfall of rotted trees, the same distant mountain peaks that were visible here and there through the breaks in the forest.

Then one day, about ten weeks after 8 and his family had arrived in Yellowstone National Park, everything changed. That morning, the Crystal Creek pack discovered an opening in the fence of the pen. Though 8 and his parents and brothers didn't realize it, the humans—National Park Service wolf biologists who worked at the park—had opened the gate to the enclosure. The time had come for the wolf family to begin to make their way in the great big world.

But at the gate, the wolves caught the scent of humans who'd entered the enclosure to drop off meat. Instead of leaving, the wolves stayed in the pen, their fear of humans overcoming even their desire to be free. A couple of days later, the biologists cut a hole in the fence some distance from the gate and placed a deer carcass just outside the pen. This time, the six wolves carefully eased their way out of the pen, first to feed on the dead deer and then to explore their new home beyond the fenced enclosure. They didn't go far on that first day. The wolves had grown used to the enclosure. For more than two months it had been their home, and now they were unsure what they should do. In fact, ten days passed before the Crystal Creek pack left the security of their enclosure for good, and four weeks before they began to fully explore their section of the park. Finally, they began to behave in the way they had before their capture—the way wolves had always behaved. And for the first time in seven decades wolves roamed freely in Yellowstone National Park.

Established in 1872, Yellowstone National Park was the first national park in both the United States and the world. Famous for its Old Faithful geyser, Yellowstone covers 3,468 square miles (8,982 square kilometers). It is largely located in northwestern Wyoming but spills over into Montana and Idaho. ★ RICK

It was early morning several days after 8 and his family had moved away from their acclimation pen. In a small meadow surrounded by tall pines, they came across an old elk carcass. Both 8's mom, the alpha female 5, and his dad, the alpha male 4, lifted a back leg and peed on a nearby bush, then scratched the site with their hind legs. The peeing and scratching sent a message, thanks to the scent glands wolves have between their toe pads. Any other wolves that happened into the area would know right away that this territory belonged to two alpha wolves and to steer clear.

That done, Wolf 5 led the pack toward a big herd of bison. In wolf families, the alpha female is the leader and primary decision-maker. The parent wolves quickly realized these huge creatures were not like the elk they normally hunted and began moving away from the bison. The four pups, however, were curious. They followed a big bull as he walked toward the rest of the herd.

The bull bison stopped and looked at the wolves. The pups hesitated, then crept forward toward the 2,000-pound (900-kilogram) animal. 8 watched his brothers, careful at first not to get too far away from them as they inched closer to this massive creature. While 8 normally preferred to stay as far away from his brothers as possible, right now, with the massive bison just several feet (about a meter) away, they represented security. The bison turned and glared at the pups. One of 8's brothers dropped back, not wanting to risk getting any closer and perhaps making the bison angry. 8 thought about dropping back too, but he wanted to find out more about these giants of the woods. The three brothers continued to move forward, now with 8 in the lead. The bull turned and joined the rest of the bison and the three pups edged still closer. Several of the bison were now looking at them. Suddenly the three pups weren't quite as brave and adventurous as they had been. Even 8 was having second thoughts about how close he wanted to be to woolly beasts that looked even more fearsome up close.

8's mother and father watched intently as their pups continued to shadow the bison. Just then, the bull charged the wolf pups, sending them scurrying back to their parents. The adventure was over.

The six Crystal Creek wolves continued on their way. It wasn't long before the two adults spotted a herd of elk. Elk are large—the cows weigh approximately 500 pounds (225 kilograms) and the bulls can weigh up to 700 pounds (320 kilograms). But while they are much bigger than wolves, they are considerably smaller than bison and, as a result, are a lot more manageable as prey. Back in Alberta, 8's parents had specialized in hunting elk.

As the wolves advanced, the elk ran off. The wolves didn't give chase but moved slowly forward. The elk in Yellowstone National Park had never seen wolves, and they were curious. How dangerous were these new-comers? The elk stopped running, turned, and walked toward the wolves. When they got to within 50 yards (45 meters) or so of where 8 and his family were stand-ing, the elk apparently decided the wolves were a threat after all. They ran off, the hundreds of hooves a drum-ming thunder on the frozen ground. Two of 8's brothers took off in pursuit. The elk split into two groups and one of the wolf pups abandoned the chase. When the sec-ond group of elk stopped running, the other wolf pup decided he, too, would rejoin his family.

Throughout all the starting and stopping, chasing and retreating, the two alpha wolves, 8's mother and father, hadn't joined their sons. Instead, they seemed to be studying the elk to see if there was one that was injured or sick, one that might provide an opportunity for a kill. They knew that healthy elk are faster than wolves and didn't want to waste their time and energy chasing them. Instead, they'd wait for a slower animal that was showing signs of weakness for one reason or another.

On this day there was no weaker elk lagging at the back of the pack, and 8's parents decided to abandon the hunt. They knew there'd be another day, another oppor-tunity to do what was needed to feed themselves and their growing family. And through it all, 8 had also been watching and learning. He was beginning to acquire the skills and knowledge he would need throughout his life. He learned, too, that there would be days when there was no kill. On those days 8, his parents, and his brothers would be hungry. And they would stay hungry until a kill was made. That was part of being a wolf.

◇ ◇ ◇

The Crystal Creek wolves were not alone in the section of Yellowstone that made up their home. There were other animals, of course, but there were also humans. Among them were the rangers and biologists whose job it was to observe 8 and his family and the other wolves that had been released into Yellowstone National Park.

One of those rangers was Rick McIntyre. Rick was born in Lowell, Massachusetts. He and his family lived in an old schoolhouse right next to the woods, ponds, and fields that he came to love. He spent countless hours fishing in those ponds, hiking in those woods, and biking the back roads. The more time Rick spent outdoors, the more he became interested in the wildlife he saw around him. The fish he caught weren't for the dinner table. Instead, Rick liked to keep them in a small aquarium. He caught turtles too, and after examining each one, he'd set them free.

A nearby farm had two dogs; their names were Rex and Shepy. Rick had noticed that Shepy liked to wander off into the woods and come back late at night, just like

Rick did. One morning Rick set out to follow Shepy and see what he was up to. He spent the day trailing along after the dog as it explored the woods, sniffing here and there and investigating the trails that wound their way through the forest. That day of following, observing, and studying Shepy was a preview of what Rick would spend his life doing. Except that instead of following an inquisitive farm dog out to see the world, Rick would devote his life to studying wild wolves.

Rick studied forestry at the University of Massachusetts and, after graduating, went to work in Alaska at Mount McKinley National Park (now known as Denali National Park and Preserve). There he guided visitors on nature walks and gave evening campfire talks, telling people about the area and the animals that lived there.

The park's grizzly population was the main attraction to visitors, and Rick, too, was fascinated by the magnificent bears, as well as caribou, moose, Dall sheep, and the many bird species that lived in that part of the world.

But even then, Rick's greatest wish was to see a wolf. They were rare in the park and seldom seen. But one day Rick's long-held wish came true as he was able to observe two gray wolves as they stalked a cow moose and her two calves. Those were the first wolves he had ever seen in the wild, and the experience made it even more clear to Rick that he wanted to see more of them and study what their lives were like.

For the next fourteen summers he returned to Denali and saw and learned more about wolves. Eventually he wrote a book about wolves, and soon after was offered a job as the wolf interpreter at Yellowstone National Park. The year was 1994. The planning for the long-awaited reintroduction of wolves to Yellowstone National Park was in its final stages. The wolves were scheduled to arrive in January 1995. Rick's job was to explain the reintroduction plan to visitors and describe what Yellowstone would be like when wolves were restored to the park.

And although Rick wasn't there to welcome them to their new home, he soon became one of the people who would observe and record their behavior. Over the next three decades, he devoted himself to telling the world the remarkable story of Wolf 8 and the other wolves of Yellowstone Park.

The Grizzly

Every day was a new experience for 8 and his brothers, filled with the lessons that would allow them to survive and thrive as adult wolves in Yellowstone National Park. And while all four brothers were taking in everything their parents could teach them, 8 was also getting good at learning things on his own.

This particular day was no different. It was spring, and though the days were longer now, the warmth that would soon come to Yellowstone had not yet arrived. 8 was alone and traveling through the part of the park called Lamar Valley. 8 often traveled by himself, partly because his brothers still sometimes ganged up on him. 8 had no way of knowing it, but he'd just had his first birthday. That meant he was no longer a pup but a yearling, which made him about the same age as a human twelve-year-old.

Sometimes it's said that no two species are more alike than wild wolves and human beings. The proof of that is how well the domestic version of the wolf—the pet dog— fits into the human family. Like humans, wolves live in extended families, they support themselves, they rescue each other if they're in danger, and they use teamwork to earn their living and raise their pups. They're very similar to us, and that's why I'm especially fascinated by them.

One term you have already encountered and will see a lot more of in this book is *alpha*. The alpha male and female are the highest-ranking wolves within the pack. But the leader of the pack is the alpha female, a critical job requiring intelligence, leadership skills, and courage. Alpha female wolves are tremendously important to the success of the pack. *Beta* females and males are secondary to the alphas. ★ RICK

It wasn't long before he spotted something hunkered down in a meadow. 8 trotted over to check it out and spied a massive bison bull, bedded down. For a long moment, 8 kept still, studying the beast. He remembered his and his brothers' encounter with a similar bison bull a few months before, and again it was his curiosity that drove him to check out this gigantic creature.

It was strange looking with its shaggy, dark brown coat, its enormous head and horns, and great humped back. This was the first time 8 had come upon a bison when he was by himself, and he decided to take a closer look. He dropped down into a crouch and eased forward, wanting to sneak up on the bison, occasionally sniffing and moving back and forth, all the while being careful to stay behind the bison. He wasn't really afraid, but he was being cautious. He was quite sure it wouldn't be a good idea to anger one of these. This thing was *huge*, more than twenty times the size of a wolf yearling. Yes, caution was definitely the best approach.

Still, 8 wasn't ready to abandon his investigation of what might be prey. He remained behind the bull, watching, waiting, and trying to decide what to do next. He took another step closer. At that exact moment, the bison flicked his tail at a fly that was irritating him. Then he flicked his tail again. And again. That was enough for 8. He took one last look and then ran off. It was one thing to be brave; it was quite another to be stupid. And 8 wasn't stupid.

He rejoined his family, and together the six Crystal Creek wolves continued their travel through Lamar Valley. But it wasn't long before 8 and two of his brothers wandered off; soon, they were enjoying the chasing game, one of the games they loved to play. But there was a difference in those games now. When they were younger, 8's brothers had taken turns beating up on him, but that was no longer the case. The little gray—the underdog—was now able to hold his own with all of his bigger brothers.

The game went on. First one yearling, then another would jump on one of his brothers and then run off with the other in hot pursuit. Suddenly, though, the game stopped. All three young wolves stared hard at a nearby stand of trees; there was something in there. They weren't sure what it was, but they wanted to find out—*right now*. 8's brothers charged forward. 8 hesitated, but only for a few seconds. He wasn't about to be left out of whatever excitement might be waiting for them. Once in the stand of trees, 8 took a second to get his bearings. Then he spotted his brothers racing back and forth, trying to get hold of a dead elk calf that was lying between a couple of pine trees. 8 jumped ahead, ready to help. That's when he realized he and his brothers weren't alone in that grove of trees. The kill belonged to the one that had killed it. And *that* was a large, very angry grizzly bear.

First one brother and then the other lunged at the dead calf, trying to grab it while staying out of range of the bear's massive jaws and huge, deadly paws. 8 joined the action, growling, snarling, and charging forward, then leaping back as the enraged grizzly snapped and swiped at the three brothers.

And then—success! One of the brothers snagged the dead calf and raced out of the trees. The second black yearling bolted out of the timber, right behind his brother, both of them running as if their lives depended on getting out of there—fast!

They were right. Their lives *did* depend on it. Seeing his brothers on the run, 8 figured it was time for him to make his escape. He, too, raced out of the stand of trees, but he was well behind his brothers. Then a fourth animal emerged from the trees—the very large, very *unhappy* grizzly bear. It was clearly upset that the wolves had made off with its dinner.

The grizzly was gaining on 8. If it caught up to him, it would make short work of this annoying little thief. 8 knew that, but he also knew he didn't really like running away from anything, not even something as ferocious as an infuriated grizzly.

Then something totally unexpected happened. 8 suddenly stopped running and turned to face the bear. And though he was just a fraction of the bear's size, 8 growled, snarled, and bared his teeth. And he stood his ground. His brothers, still carrying the dead calf, had continued on and disappeared over a hill. They had escaped to safety. Now it was one small yearling wolf and one large grizzly bear in a standoff, neither of them inclined to back off.

The bear came closer. Now it was just several feet (about a meter) away from the small gray wolf. It seemed undecided about what to do. 8 may have been little compared to the bear, but he was clearly unafraid. In fact, he actually looked confident.

The two stared at one another for a long time. Finally, 8 turned and casually trotted off. The bear sniffed the ground, then the air, and, unable to figure out where the other wolves and the dead calf had gone, turned and wandered back in the direction it had come from.

None of his brothers had seen what happened between 8 and the grizzly. They hadn't witnessed the courage of the brother they had so often picked on. They would never know what went on while they made their escape from a large and dangerous enemy. But 8 now knew that he was capable of accomplishing great things. As his brothers settled down to feed on the stolen calf carcass, 8 took up his place at the dinner table right alongside them. The little gray that had once been picked on and beaten down had taken another step toward becoming an alpha male.

Years after observing Wolf 8 and the grizzly, I heard actor Dwayne Johnson, who often plays a hero in his movies, speak about real-life heroes. He said, "Being a hero means doing the right thing, even when no one is watching." I had witnessed 8's heroism. And I was reminded of something that was said to Frodo in the movie adaptation of J. R. R. Tolkien's *The Fellowship of the Ring*, in the Lord of the Rings trilogy: "Even the smallest person can change the course of the future." I vowed to share the story of 8's encounter with the grizzly with as many people as possible, especially with kids who have been having a hard time in life. 8's actions showed that both Dwayne Johnson and the *Fellowship* movie were right: even the smallest individual can be a big hero. ★ RICK

◇ ◇ ◇

Many miles away from the Crystal Creek pack's territory, at about the same time as 8's family was leaving their pen, another pack was bedding down for the night. They were the Rose Creek pack, and the mother, Wolf 9, had given birth to a litter of eight pups just a few days before. Those pups were the first born in the Yellowstone area since the 1920s.

One of those pups was Wolf 21, although he was still too young to have been given a number. He was a black male who liked to burrow into the den, worming his way past his brothers and sisters to the warmest spot—the back corner, snuggled up against his mother. It was the perfect place. He felt warm there, and safe. But there was a problem. He had seven brothers and sisters! All of them wanted to get as close to their mother as he did, and there wasn't always enough room. But 21 didn't give up easily. Most of the time, he was able to secure his favorite spot next to his mom, who often gave her persistent son a welcoming lick. 21 would then lay his head on his paws and drop off to sleep.

The eight little pups curled up at the back of the den and the mother wolf were not aware that something terrible had happened just a few days before. In fact, it happened on the very day 21 was born. At almost the exact same time that his mother was having her litter of pups, their father was off on a hunt about 5 miles

(8 kilometers) away. The den was not far from the town of Red Lodge, Montana. Sadly, while Wolf 10 was trying to hunt elk to feed his family, he ventured into an area quite close to the town and was illegally shot and killed. The man who shot him was eventually charged with killing an animal protected under the Endangered Species Act, and he spent time in jail.

The death of Wolf 10 changed everything for this pack. Wolf 9 was now a widow who had eight pups to look after all by herself. Newborn wolf pups cannot regulate their own body temperature and have to snuggle up against their parents to stay warm. But in this case, there was only one parent, and eventually she would have to leave the pups to hunt for food. And when she did, anything could happen. In fact, there was a good chance the pups would die, either from the cold or from a predator, such as a coyote, that they would be helpless to defend themselves against.

The young pup who would one day be called 21 didn't know that humans had located the site and were planning to capture his mother and all her pups. Unlike the man who had killed his father, these humans were there to help. The biologists knew that if they could get 9 and her brood back to their acclimation pen, their chances of survival would greatly increase.

Jarred awake by his brothers and sisters whimpering and running back and forth, the pup raced out of the den to see what was going on. Humans were nearby, and while 21 did not know it, they'd already captured his mother. The pups continued to whimper and scurry back and forth, wanting to be with their mother, but in the end their fear of the humans drove them back into the den. All, that is, except for one black pup. He stood his ground, staring hard and growling at the intruders until finally even he dashed back into the chamber that was embedded in a jumble of rocks. One member of the rescue team carefully reached into the den and extracted first one pup, then another, until he had seven pups caught.

With the rescue all but completed, the man had a hunch there might be one more pup. And sure enough, he was right. There was one last snarling, miniature ball of fury deep inside the den. The little black pup struggled and fought, determined not to be forced from his hiding place. But finally, the human prevailed. The scrappy three-week-old was pulled out into the sunlight. It was the same pup who moments before had bravely tried to face down the invaders.

The wolf family was loaded onto a helicopter and flown to the Rose Creek acclimation pen, the site where 9 and 10 had lived for two months prior to being released. The plan was for Wolf 9 and her eight pups to spend six months in the enclosure, until the pups were big enough to have a good chance for survival once they were released. During that time the wolves would be safe and their mother would not have to leave them to go off to hunt. As they had done with the Crystal Creek pack, the biologists brought carcasses to the wolf family twice a week, then quickly left so that the wolves would not become unnaturally attached to their human caregivers.

The man who pulled out the pup who eventually became known as Wolf 21 from deep inside the den was Doug Smith, a Yellowstone wolf biologist. Working on a hunch that one more pup was still inside, he reached as far into the den as he could, with no luck. Other people on the scene told Doug that they had to leave, and that he should give up, but he kept at it. He got a stick and poked around the den. In one spot, the stick touched something soft. That spot was too far back for Doug to reach, so he got a pair of pliers and gently grabbed the object. As he pulled that last pup forward it struggled to stay in the den with all its strength, but Doug was stronger. He dragged the pup out into the open and placed him in the container that held his mother and seven brothers and sisters.

A veterinarian named Mark Johnson was also on the scene that day, in case any of the wolves needed medical attention. Mark is an expert at recognizing dogs, wolves, and other animals as they grow up to adult size. Later on, he realized that last pup—the one that almost got left behind—was the one who grew up to be Wolf 21. ★ RICK

When the biologists brought the elk and moose carcasses to the pen, 9 and her pups would back away to
the far side. But sometimes, one pup would do something very different. Little 21 would step away from
his mother and the other pups, walk forward, and place
himself between them and the humans. Like a miniature alpha male, he paced back and forth between the
people and his family. He didn't growl or threaten the
intruders. But 21 let them know he was there, and that if
they wanted to get to his family, they would have to go
through him first.

> **What was amazing about 21's behavior was that his father,
> Wolf 10, had done exactly the same thing before he was
> killed. While 10 and 9 were in the enclosure, 10 would take
> up that same position between the humans and his family
> and he would pace back and forth. Now here was his son,
> who had never known his father, emulating that protective
> behavior, and sending the same message his father had.**
> ★ **RICK**

3

The New Family

Fall had come to Yellowstone. Temperatures cooled, leaves fell from trees, and the days grew shorter, all signs of the approaching winter.

Something else was about to change in the park too. It was something very important, and somewhat worrisome, to the rangers and biologists. It was time for Wolf 9 and her pups to be released from their acclimation pen. There was good reason for the concern. Even though the pups were older and bigger now, the chances that a lone female wolf could look after eight hungry pups and keep them and herself alive and well were slim indeed. But sometimes in nature, miracles happen.

◇ ◇ ◇

Not far away from the Rose Creek pen, a stranger was making his way up a creek drainage. 8 was wandering, as he often did, by himself. Hunting, exploring, checking out the sights and sounds, 8, who was still a yearling but a bit older (a teenager in human years), was totally comfortable moving through Yellowstone on his own. Partway through his explorations, he came to a large meadow where the green of summer was now being replaced by the browns and yellows of autumn.

He was in no hurry. He moved slowly through the meadow, stopping occasionally to check the smells of this fallen log or that rock pile. Then he stopped dead in his tracks, on full alert. He'd heard something—a sound he knew very well. Not far away, a wolf, maybe more than one, was howling. In fact, the howling was coming from the far end of the meadow.

At first 8 was cautious. Crouching, waiting, watching. Then he saw the wolves that had been making the noise. Wolf pups. Quite a lot of wolf pups. 8 stared at them, not fully understanding what he was seeing. He had never before seen wolves that were smaller than he was. Perhaps he remembered his own time as a young pup, when his father would play with him. And with that memory might have come another—a memory of his brothers constantly pestering him, picking on him, ganging up on him.

8 approached the pups. They were as surprised as he was. Just as he'd never seen wolves this small, these pups had never encountered an older male wolf; they'd never seen a wolf this big. 8 wagged his tail and then got

down on his front paws, his rump in the air, to greet the little wolves. They returned the gesture. In the world of wolf communication, that stance—the play bow—is an invitation to play.

And play they did. Soon 8 and the Rose Creek pups were romping around the meadow like long-lost pals. At the edge of the clearing, the pups' mother, Wolf 9, was watching carefully. At first she was worried by the arrival of this gray stranger, but the sight of him playing with her pups reassured her that he wasn't a threat. She desperately needed an adult male in her family to help raise her pups, so she eventually came forward to meet the wolf who was clearly a big hit. At first, she cautiously joined in the play. Then she and 8 came face to face for the first time, their faces and muzzles touching as they made little whining sounds of greeting. Finally, 8 placed a paw on 9's shoulder. He liked this wolf, liked her a lot. And as they looked at and gently touched each other, 8 made a decision, one of the most important of his entire life.

Wolf 8 would not return to his mother and father and brothers. He had found a new family and had been accepted into it by Wolf 9 and all of her pups. But as important as deciding to become part of a new family was, it was still the easy part. The changes 8 would be making as a result of that decision would be anything but easy. He was taking on a huge responsibility, especially difficult and demanding for so young a male wolf. It had only been a year since he had been the smallest, most picked-on wolf pup in Yellowstone, and now here he was adopting eight fatherless pups that he would raise as if they were his own. The wolf who had been the little underdog was now the alpha male in a ten-wolf pack.

◇ ◇ ◇

A few weeks had passed since 8 and his new family had come together. Winter was settling in all through Yellowstone National Park. The first snows had turned the meadows white and the temperatures were dropping. 8 and his adopted family were traveling the woods and meadows hunting for elk or other prey animals, something they could take down that would provide meat for the large family.

But the animal they encountered wasn't prey. It was one of 8's brothers, now a large yearling and potentially a threat. Wolf 9 took the threat seriously and raced forward to attack the intruder. 8 did not hesitate. He joined his mate and immediately took the fight to his brother, one of the bullies who'd beaten him up as a young pup.

None of that mattered now. His family was under threat and 8 would not allow that threat to go unchallenged. Instantly, he transformed into a warrior—

snarling, biting, throwing his body again and again into the larger wolf that had once enjoyed the role of big brother. The big black wolf fought back but was no match for the fury of 8's attack.

In this fight their former roles were reversed. It was the bigger brother that ran off, his tail between his legs and with 8 in hot pursuit. He had to make sure the intruder would not return. 8 chased his brother for a while, until he was satisfied the threat to his family had been eliminated. Then he trotted back to rejoin 9 and his adopted pups.

It was a hero's welcome. The pups licked 8's face and 9 jumped on his back. 8 enjoyed the attention. He looked affectionately at his mate, then at each of the pups... *his* pups. If there had been any doubt about 8's ability to look after his mate and the pups he had adopted, that doubt had, at least for the moment, been laid to rest. Wolf 8 had proven himself: he was an alpha male who would do whatever was needed to protect his family.

◇ ◇ ◇

There would soon be further challenges to 8's ability as an alpha male. Trouble was brewing in Lamar Valley. That winter, more wolves arrived in Yellowstone National Park from the Canadian province of British Columbia as part of the repopulation program. One of the packs would come to be known as the Druid pack. The pack consisted of a female, Wolf 39, whose mate had been killed, her three daughters (40, 41, and 42), and an unrelated male, Wolf 38, who would be introduced to the female and her pups in their acclimation pen.

Wolf 38 was huge and remarkably strong. During the trip from Canada to Yellowstone he ripped apart the metal cage he'd been placed in and wandered around inside the trailer. He finally had to be tranquilized and put in a stronger cage for the last part of the trip. The Druids eventually arrived safely at Yellowstone and soon were put in their acclimation pen for the winter, the same pen that had been used by 9 and her family.

The pairing of Wolf 38 and the female 39 worked out well, and when spring rolled around once more, they were released as the other packs had been. But there was a problem. Though there was plenty of unoccupied wolf territory for this new pack to establish itself in, the Druids settled in Lamar Valley, not far from the Crystal Creek pack, which now consisted of 8's parents and one of 8's brothers. They were also near the Rose Creek pack that had just seen 8's mate, Wolf 9, give birth to three pups, making 8 a biological father for the first time. 9's pups from the previous year were now yearlings, and they would be helping their mother and 8 raise and protect the newborn pups.

It was inevitable that these packs would one day meet. And it was likely that when they did, there would be a fight for supremacy. It wasn't long before the powerful male, 38, and his family encountered the Crystal Creek pack and the den where 8's mother had just had a litter of pups. The Druids attacked the Crystal Creek wolves and killed the newborn pups. 8's father, Wolf 4, tried to protect his family, but he was no match for the massive and vicious Wolf 38. Wolf 4 was killed, leaving only the female Wolf 5 and a yearling male, brother to Wolf 8, as survivors.

> I mentioned earlier that one of the reasons wolves have always fascinated me is the similarity of wolf and human behavior. The showdown between Wolf 38 and Wolf 4 is another example, though not a very pleasant one. Both species frequently fight over things, and sometimes they kill each other. But this was a difficult time for those of us who had come to know the Crystal Creek pack over the past year. They were our home team. And now it seemed like they were about to go out of existence, since they had lost all their pups along with their alpha male and were down to just two members. And it was all due to the arrival of the Druids. Park visitors began to refer to them as the "bad wolves of Lamar." It was as if a band of outlaws had ridden into town and taken over. ★ RICK

◇ ◇ ◇

Meanwhile, Wolf 8 was working hard raising three newborn pups, and he seemed to enjoy being a new dad. Of course, he had adopted Wolf 9's pups the year before, but this was different. For one thing, he had been there from the birth of these new pups and seen them from their first days. He knew that he was charged with going out on hunts and bringing the meat back to the den his mate, 9, had dug out at a site called Mom's Ridge for herself and the new litter.

But there was an ongoing responsibility as well. It was 8's job to teach his adopted sons and daughters how to hunt elk. On one warm spring day, it was time for lessons to begin. 8 led his charges away from the den in search of suitable prey. They encountered a herd of elk not far from Slough Creek, and 8 ran toward it. With the help of several yearlings he killed an elk calf that was much slower than all the others, a sign that it was sick or injured.

8 and the yearlings fed for a while. They were about to take some of the meat back to the den for 9 and the new pups when suddenly 8 stopped what he was doing. He raised his head and looked off toward a nearby ridge. This time, it wasn't elk that had caught his attention. It was the Druid wolf pack, and they were racing down the slope directly at 8 and the yearlings. Leading the Druids' charge was 38, the wolf that was so strong he had ripped apart a metal cage, the wolf that had killed 8's father.

Instantly, 8 was off and running at top speed—not away from the massive 38 and the outlaw Druids, but directly at them. This would be the most difficult challenge of 8's young life. When 8 had driven off his brother the previous winter, he had fought a wolf that was his age. Although his brother was bigger than him, 8 was not nearly as big as the wolf that was leading the charge down the hill. 38 wasn't just big, he was also older, and he was a skilled and ferocious fighter. He would show no mercy either to 8 or, once he had disposed of their adoptive father, to the yearlings.

If 8 knew or sensed the danger, or realized that the odds were heavily stacked against him, it didn't seem to matter. He ran straight uphill at 38, ears back and teeth bared. His speed never wavered as he bore closer to the massive wolf coming at him. 8 also didn't care about the size of his opponent. He didn't know about 38's previous victories and feats of strength, and wouldn't have hesitated for even a second if he had. And he didn't care that his adversary was running downhill while he was running up the hill and would be tired when the two warriors came together. This was an enemy and a threat to his family, and 8 knew only one thing—he would do whatever it took, no matter the cost, to protect his pack.

The two alpha males crashed together in a furious frenzy of growls, snarls, and snapping jaws. Both 8 and 38 were gray, and the two wolves quickly became one mass of savage fury. For the first seconds of the fight neither wolf gained an advantage. The fight raged on, first one, then the other on top, but still it was impossible to tell if either was winning. Then, as suddenly as it had begun, it was over. One of the gray wolves was standing over the other, holding him down and biting the defeated wolf over and over.

The wolf standing over his beaten enemy was 8. The wolf that as a yearling had faced down a grizzly, then fought off one of his bigger brothers when his new family was in danger, had just encountered the greatest challenge of his young life, and he had been victorious. When alpha males fight, the battle is often to the death, with the victor standing over the defeated—powerful jaws inflicting pain and damage until the loser is dead. It's impossible to know if 8 sensed that the wolf he had just fought had killed his father. Still, he had taken down an opponent that had been intent on destroying his family, and in the wild world of Yellowstone, he would have been justified in ending the life of that brutal foe.

But no wolves would die on this day. 8 stepped back and allowed 38 to get up. He had won the fight and saved his family. And for 8 that was enough. He didn't need to kill his adversary. Maybe he didn't *want* to kill his adversary.

The big wolf tucked his tail and ran off. To establish his dominance more clearly, 8 chased him and the other Druids up and over the ridge, making sure they were gone for good. Then he returned to the yearlings, who excitedly jumped all over him in a victory celebration.

I've thought about the fight between 8 and 38 many times over the years. Eventually, I came up with the theory that 8 had learned a lot about how a wolf can lose a fight during all those times his brothers had beaten him up. If you remember how you lost a fight, you can also remember how your opponent won. I think 8 recalled what his brothers had done to beat him, reversed it, and used it to throw 38 to the ground and defeat him. That means that the bullying he endured as a pup may have saved his life. And as for his sparing the life of his adversary that day, that pattern continued for the rest of 8's long life: as far as we know, he never killed a defeated opponent.

One of the yearlings out on the hunt with 8 that day was Wolf 21. He watched as his adoptive father defeated 38 and then spared his life. I would later learn what a profound influence 8's behavior had on his adopted son's life.

★ RICK

Good Wolf, Bad Wolf

It was a warm day under a cloudless sky, and 8 was in a lazy mood.

He'd been busy, what with hunting and fighting off other wolves to protect his family. Today's hunt had been successful, and after an enthusiastic and affectionate greeting from the pups, just like he received every time he arrived home, 8 lay down to rest and watch his family at play.

He enjoyed these days. He liked spending time with his mate and the pups—both the adopted pups, who were now yearlings, and the three pups Wolf 9 had given birth to just a few weeks before. Wolf 17, one of 8's adopted daughters, was an especially playful youngster. The gray female pranced over to one of her brothers and performed the play bow, dropping her front end to the ground and keeping her back end in the air. Her brother immediately recognized the invitation to play and leaped to the challenge. But he was no match for his mischievous sister. She was much faster, and she easily bounded away, only to turn back and run circles around her brother—a wolf's way of showing off.

Then another of the female yearlings joined in the fun and wrestled with her brother, the two of them playfully nipping at one another. It wasn't long before the little pups wanted to get in on the games too. And just like in human families, the older siblings loved playing with their little sister and two brothers. One yearling picked up a bone and gave it to one of the younger pups like it was a toy. And that's exactly what it was. A wolf toy.

When the young pups got tired, one of the yearlings would take the bone, flip it in the air, and catch it. And the game was on again. Keep-away, catch me if you can, and wrestling were some of the young wolves' favorite games, with an occasional break to pursue a couple of sandhill cranes and then a flock of Canada geese.

8 had been watching it all from a distance, but now he, too, wanted to join in the fun. He chased first one pup, then another, and once he'd caught them he'd run away, with the pups now in pursuit. After a few seconds he'd slow down so the pups could catch him. He'd roll onto his back and allow the pups to jump on and wrestle him for a while. Then he'd leap up and the chase would continue. Finally, tired but happy, 8 lay down again, not

far away, to watch his family at play and to keep an eye out for intruders. Then, after first allowing her three young pups to nurse, it was 9's turn to join in.

It isn't unusual for bigger and older wolves to let smaller ones win. Sometimes they just want to keep the game going, but they also genuinely care about other members of their family and are willing to occasionally give them the upper hand.

I once got to experience the way wolves play firsthand. My friend Bill owned a wolf-dog mix named Kintla. Kintla was a big, tough-looking animal, and most people were initially afraid of him. One day I was in Bill's house with Kintla, and we began a game of chase around the dining room table. Kintla chased me, but I could see he was deliberately running slower than normal, and he never actually caught me. Finally, I stopped and looked back at him. Kintla stopped too, then turned and ran the other way. I took that as an invitation to chase him.

As I ran around that table, Kintla repeatedly looked over his shoulder at me, making sure I was still playing along. We both stopped again and looked at each other; then it was his turn to chase me once more. I knew he could catch and pin me any moment he chose. Kintla knew that too, but he wanted to play and pretended to be afraid of me to prolong the fun. Those minutes I spent playing with Kintla were the closest I ever came to experiencing what it might actually be like to be a wolf. ★ RICK

Wolves are among nature's most playful animals. Winter, spring, summer, and fall, in all kinds of weather, at any time of day or night, 8 and the rest of the growing Rose Creek pack were always ready to have fun. As the leader of the game-players, 8 demonstrated his love for family and fun again later that year. Winter had set in with a vengeance and dumped major amounts of snow on much of Yellowstone. But 8 wasn't about to let a little nasty weather get in the way. When the snow let up a bit, he led the whole family to the top of a nearby steep hill, where they took turns sliding down.

> Those views of 8's family and his new pups were some of the best wolf sightings I've ever had. They were so much like human parents and brothers and sisters, and I was reminded again of the similarities between wolves and humans, especially in the way they relate to each other.
> ★ RICK

◇ ◇ ◇

Not every wolf is the same. And not every pack operates the same way. Wolves have individual personalities, and those personalities have an effect on other members of the pack. The Druid pack, for instance, was very different from the Crystal Creek and Rose Creek packs—and it was all because of one member. Wolf 38, the huge male who had been defeated by the smaller 8, was still powerful and aggressive, but he wasn't the dominant force in his pack.

Wolf 40 was a yearling female from 39's previous litter, meaning she had been born in Canada. She had a violent, aggressive personality. She turned on her mother and drove her out of the family. And after that, she repeatedly beat up her two sisters, 41 and 42. It was clear she wanted to force them to leave the family as well.

40 was now the undisputed alpha female in the Druid pack, and under her reign, the Druids earned a reputation as a ruthless, bloodthirsty band. But under the surface, there was more to this family. Though 38 was huge and remarkably strong, he was just as play-ful and gentle with his pups as other alpha males like 8. And as a pack, the Druids could be very resourceful.

Although Wolf 39 had been driven from the pack by her disagreeable daughter, she was allowed to return for a time, and in the spring of 1997 was assisting with the care of the young pups, her grandchildren. On one par-ticularly hot July day, four Druid adults and four pups were traveling downhill through a meadow when they came to a road that wasn't far from their den. 39 and the two alpha wolves, 38 and 40, crossed the road and continued on their way. But the pups stopped to sniff all the interesting smells on the pavement. Luckily, no vehi-cles came along right then. The adult wolves, who had gone farther south, finally turned back to check on the pups' progress. And when they saw the pups still milling around on the road, they raced back.

When 38 reached his pups, he trotted right past them and up the hill toward the meadow. As the pups followed along, 40 remained on the road until all were safely clear. 39, the grandmother, and Wolf 41, the fourth adult on the outing, led the pups still farther away from the danger of the road. On this day, teamwork among the adult Druids helped avoid what could have been a dangerous situation for the pups.

Constant Companions

Things were changing in 8's life.

He was three years old in the spring of 1997, and his mate, Wolf 9, had given birth to seven pups, three blacks and four grays. It was the second litter of pups that 8 had fathered. That April was a busy time for the mother and father. But that wasn't the only change for 8.

Ever since he was a pup, 8 had always preferred spending time by himself. It was better than being ganged up on, bullied by his brothers, or having his food taken from him. But now that he was an adult and a father, he no longer felt quite the same way. He liked spending time with his mate. And, of course, there were new pups to raise, but 8 now had lots of help from the young adults in the family: the two-year-olds he had adopted as well as the yearlings he'd fathered the previous spring. But it was one young wolf in particular that was changing 8's "loner" attitude—Wolf 21.

Over the past twelve months, 21 had become an almost inseparable companion to 8. He was two years old now and had grown to be much bigger than his adoptive father. But despite the difference in their sizes, there was never any doubt who was in charge. 8 was the leader and 21 his loyal, willing, and very capable apprentice.

Like all wolves, 8 liked to start his day at first light, about half an hour before sunrise. And this particular day was no different. 8 woke first, stretched, yawned, and wandered quietly around the area where 9 had established a den. It had rained the night before, but with morning the sun came out and began to dry the damp ground and warm the forest's cool air.

8 was soon joined by 21 and, as was often the case, the younger pups also appeared and fell in next to their big brother. They licked his face and he gave them some small pieces of meat from a recent elk kill. 8 watched as 21 tolerated his new half-siblings being underfoot and in the way. The patience he showed toward the smaller wolves was just one of the lessons 21 had learned from his father.

As the wolves ate, a raven landed and tried to steal some of the meat. It almost got away with it too, thanks to 21 being busy with the pups and not really paying attention. But 8 was on the lookout, and ready. He chased the bird away before it could make off with any of the food. After allowing 21 a little more time with the younger pups, 8 let his adopted son know it was time to head off on a hunt. They were a unique pair, the smaller gray wolf and the younger, larger black one, and they were often spotted together as they ranged near and far in search of food.

On this day, it wasn't long before the two hunters spotted a small group of elk and gave chase. 8 took the lead. Charging ahead, he was able to get in front of a 300-pound (135-kilogram) cow elk. He leaped up and grabbed her by the throat, knowing he could count on 21 to do exactly what was needed next. And he was right. As 8 hung on to the elk's throat, 21 bit into one of the cow's hind legs. The cow was so strong she lifted 8 completely off the ground. As he had done so many times, 8 was once again facing a much larger opponent—and once again he was determined not to give up. He hung on for dear life, even as he dangled in midair.

With 8's grip cutting off her air supply, the elk eventually collapsed. Father and son had demonstrated the teamwork they would show over and over as they looked after their growing family. When the successful hunters returned to the den area, 21 carried a big piece of meat to his mother while 8 gathered the hungry young pups around him and regurgitated food for them.

Wolf parents will often feed their pups by regurgitation—
that is, bringing food they have stored in their stomachs
back up into their mouths and then spitting it out onto the
ground for the pups to eat. The pups will run to the returning hunters and lick their faces. The licking will trigger the
regurgitation, which is not the same as nausea or throwing
up. The adults are not sick; they are just providing food for
the youngest members of the family. When pet dogs lick
the faces of their human friends when they return home, it
is a reminder that their distant ancestors were wolves.

★ RICK

Quickly, though, 8 and 21 realized something was wrong. Only six pups came out of the den to greet them and dive into the food. One pup, gray, almost tan in color, didn't come forward to feed with the others. He stayed back and seemed to be sick. He even fell a few times.

21 left his other siblings and trotted up to the tan pup. 21 was tired from the hunt, and from carrying the large piece of meat back to the den. On another day, he might have rested after his hard work. Instead, he sat down beside the tan pup, nuzzling him and just hanging out—a big brother caring about his little brother.

A few days later, 21 was bedded down next to a big boulder. It was quiet in the woods but he was restless, watchful. Suddenly, he jumped up and raced off to drive away a bear that had come dangerously close to the den. When 21 returned, the six healthy pups came out to greet him. Then, a few minutes later, the tan pup stood up, wagged his tail, and pranced happily down the hill, even climbing over a log as he hurried to join 21 and the others. It seemed as if 21's caring concern had worked wonders.

Wolf 9's den was visible from the park road, which allowed me to watch the interaction between 21 and the sick pup. I was impressed by what I'd seen. Imagine you had a hard day at school. Now imagine how you'd feel if your dog ran over to greet you the minute you got home. That would cheer you up, right? Well, a dog's ability to have empathy for a human friend—meaning they understand when we are sad or need help—comes directly from their wolf ancestors. And a wolf like 21 probably learned the empathy and caring he showed his brother from his dad, Wolf 8.

Over the years, I have been asked by the Make-A-Wish Foundation to take children out to see wolves. Those days when I get to help kids have a good time and forget their troubles are the best days of the year for me—and they always make me remember what I saw 21 do that day with his little brother.

There are so many stories to share about the caring nature of wolves. Years before I began working at Yellowstone, I did some presentations with Kent Weber and Tracy Ane Brooks, good friends who run Mission: Wolf, a nonprofit sanctuary for abandoned or mistreated captive-born wolves. They had a female wolf named Rami who was comfortable around people, and they took her to elementary schools when they did programs about wolves. Kent would bring the leashed Rami onstage and announce that if the students were well behaved, he would allow Rami to walk around the room so they could get a closer look. There was just one important rule: they were not allowed to touch her. But Kent explained that occasionally Rami would pick out a child she wanted to meet. If that happened, the student could pet her.

Sometimes it was a girl Rami chose to befriend, and other times a boy. It might be a young child or an older one. Kent began to ask the teachers if there was anything special about the student the wolf had chosen. The teachers nearly always said the wolf had gone to the most picked-on boy or girl in the school. Rami must have sensed the stress and sadness in those children in the same way that Wolf 21 sensed the sadness and loneliness in the little tan pup. Usually, that moment with Rami made a big difference to the student. Not only did they get to have a personal encounter with a wolf, but Rami's attention made them pretty special among their classmates, often for the very first time.

There is another story, a funnier one, about a wolf who wanted to help a human. At Wolf Haven, a sanctuary for captive-born wolves in Washington State, a young mother with a baby approached the fenced-off area where the wolves lived. As she stood there, her baby started to cry. A nearby female wolf perked up at the sound and looked at the crying baby. She then dug up an old and stinky piece of meat and shoved it under the fence so the mother could use it to feed her upset child. Another wonderful example of the caring nature of many wolves. ★ RICK

◇ ◇ ◇

Despite how caring wolves born in captivity can be in some of their interactions with people, wolves in the wild don't want anything to do with humans. The Yellowstone wolves seemed unaware of, or unconcerned about, the National Park Service biologists observing them from a distance, usually about a mile (1-2 kilometers), through high-powered spotting scopes. Mostly, the observers were there to record the various movements, behaviors, and activities of the packs. And although the researchers were happy to lend a helping hand when the wolves needed it—like when Wolf 9 had her litter of pups just after her mate had been killed—they normally did not become directly involved in the daily lives of the wolves. Keeping human interaction with the wolves to a minimum was a top priority.

But the wolves, and especially the pups, were a huge tourist attraction. People would stop their cars on their way through the park, grab their cameras and binoculars, and take every opportunity they could find to watch the wolves in their natural habitat. Occasionally, that could cause problems—which is exactly what happened one evening in May, not long after Wolf 9 had her litter of pups.

9's den was close to the road, which meant the wolves had to cross from time to time. That evening, a number of cars had stopped on the side, and the drivers and passengers watched as one adult wolf and a pup crossed the road right in front of their eyes. There was only one problem: that adult wolf—9—and her pup were now separated from the rest of the family. The rest of the pups saw people and cars between them and their mother and refused to cross the road. Seeing her distressed pups on the other side, 9 began howling encouragement to them. Something had to be done quickly—and safely—to reunite the pups with their mother.

Which is exactly when Rick stepped in. He asked the tourists to move their cars a little way down the road, just far enough to allow the wolf family room to cross without fear. All of the visitors cooperated, and when he returned to the area a little later, Mom and pups had been reunited. It was a happy ending to a situation that all too easily could have ended in tragedy.

I had a big red stop sign I'd been given by the Park Service, and occasionally I used that sign to hold up traffic so the wolves could safely cross the road. I felt like a school crosswalk monitor. I noticed that 42, one of the original daughters from the Druid pack, was the smartest of the wolves when it came to crossing. She was careful to look both ways, then scurry across if no cars were coming.

★ RICK

Love Is in the Air

That same spring, things were happening with the Druid pack.

Two of the females had become mothers that year. Sisters 41 and 42 gave birth to five pups in all, while the nasty alpha sister, Wolf 40, had not had a litter. Perhaps frustrated at not having pups of her own, she was becoming increasingly aggressive with her siblings.

On a cool morning just days after the incident with Wolf 9, her pups, and the tourists, the Druid adults left the den and set out on a hunt, with the new pups trucking dutifully along behind. The lead wolves reached a creek and waded across, but the pups stopped at the edge and howled for help. They weren't about to set a paw in the dangerous water! When the adults kept going, the howls became even more plaintive—and this time, it was 38 alone who came to his pups' rescue.

Hearing their cries, he retraced his steps to the creek. He waded into the water and quickly made his way to the far bank and to the pups, whose frightened howls faded as help arrived. 38 greeted the pups and went from one to another, spending a little time with each one until they calmed down. Then he led them back to the water's edge. Slowly, 38 waded to the other side, but this time one of the pups—a littler braver than its brothers and sisters—followed.

On the opposite bank, the whining and howling started up again. 38 and the pup that had crossed with him stood calmly and patiently on their side of the river. It was almost as if they were saying, "It's not so bad. You can do this." And finally, the four remaining pups, seeing that their father and sibling had safely navigated the creek, carefully stepped into the water and waded to the other side. Soon enough, the group caught up with the rest of the pack.

> Over the course of that spring and summer, I came to realize I might have been wrong about the Druids. Wolf 40 was clearly the pack leader. With her violent nature, she probably had been the driver of the attacks that killed 8's father and later brought 8 and 38 to their fight on the hillside. While 38 was huge and tremendously strong, he was very caring with his pups and seemed better equipped than the females in the pack to get them out of trouble. This convinced me that he was probably just a normal male wolf who had the bad luck to be in a pack led by a callous and savage alpha female. ★ RICK

◇ ◇ ◇

It was a season of change. Summer, with its warm rains and lazy, sunny days, came and went. Adults hunted and brought food for growing pups, and, as always, there was plenty of playtime in the park's wolf families. Now it was late fall and the time had come for 21, who was two and a half years old, to leave his family, find a mate, and start raising pups of his own. In Yellowstone National Park, the average life span of a wolf is five years. Some live longer, much longer—a few even reach the ripe old age of ten or eleven. But for most, life is much shorter. And that meant 21, a mature, eligible bachelor, had better get on with things.

History was about to repeat itself. Just two years had passed since a young Wolf 8 had been wandering around the forestland of Yellowstone on his own when he encountered Wolf 9 and her brood of fatherless pups. A hunter had illegally shot and killed 9's mate, and 8 joined that family and adopted 9's pups—including 21— as his own.

Now it was 21's turn to leave the family he had been with his whole life. But where would he go? 21 had become aware of Wolf 42, the beta female in the Druid pack. Although the Druid and the Rose Creek wolves kept away from each other for the most part, they occasionally moved through the same territory. It's likely that 21 had become aware of 42's scent, and it's equally possible that 42 had an idea that a young male wolf was part of that nearby pack.

There was just one problem—these two packs were rivals. When wolf families live near one another, the competition for territory, food, and den sites means that the possibility of conflict and even combat greatly increases. So, unless 21 and 42 were going to leave their packs and run off together to start a new pack (think Romeo and Juliet), there was only one way for them to get together: 21 would have to march straight into enemy territory to meet 42. Would the young male actually do it?

His decision was helped along by howling. On the other side of the road that wound its way through that section of the park, the Druid pack howled away, and the sound carried—bringing with it hints as to what kind of wolves were in the pack. As the Rose Creek wolves howled back, and the "conversation" continued, 21 figured out that there were definitely females over there. Maybe he was thinking that, with a little bit of luck, he might be able to draw off one of the females, perhaps even 42, and start a pack of his own.

And so, one day in early December, 21 headed off on his new adventure. He trotted toward the east, intent on getting close to the wolves he'd heard howling. His decision to go in that direction was potentially dangerous, and could even have been fatal. The Druids had two big males in the pack: the huge, very strong 38, who had once fought 8 while 21 looked on, and Wolf 31, who came to Yellowstone in a separate pack and later joined the Druids. There was a very real possibility that the two Druid males would see 21 as a threat and attack. But 21 was on a mission to find a mate, and he either didn't know about the pack's males or just didn't care.

He also didn't know that tragedy had just struck the Druids, forcing major changes on the pack. Both male Druids—Wolf 31 and the alpha 38—had been illegally shot outside of the park. Young 31 had quickly died of his wounds. But 38, strong to the end, clung to life. Whether driven by a desire to recover and return to his family or just because of his remarkable strength and will to live, he refused to give up. Park employees dropped meat to him, but he couldn't eat. After eleven days, the alpha male that had once been disliked by Yellowstone's human observers, but had eventually come to be respected and even admired, died.

And here's where history repeats itself. Wolf 21 was about to experience the same thing that his adoptive father, Wolf 8, had experienced some years before. With the death of its two male wolves, the Druid pack now had seven members: adult females 40 and 42, and five pups who had been born that spring. The third sister, 41, had recently been driven out by the unpleasant Wolf 40. Wolf 40 had also again driven out her mother,

Wolf 39 (who would, sadly, be illegally shot and killed the next spring).

By human standards, 40 was a beautiful wolf, mainly due to her light-colored coat. Her sister had dull-looking, dark fur that sometimes stuck out in odd places. With breeding season just a few months away, the two females and their pups needed a male to join the pack. Both 40 and 42 were looking for a mating partner, preferably a strong male to help raise the pups and protect the family.

21 and the Druids spotted one another at just about the same time. At first, concerned about their pups, 40 and 42 charged at 21, with three of the pups joining in the chase. 21 retreated a short way, but he wasn't really afraid. He hadn't come to harm them, and he could see that there were only females and pups on the scene—no adult males. So 21 stopped, turned, and looked at them. The Druid wolves also stopped, looked at 21, and howled. 21 howled back.

The pack chased him again, and again they stopped when 21 stopped. He wanted to show these wolves that he wasn't a threat, that he wasn't there to harm them. He wagged his tail, telling them he wanted to be friendly, and one of the female pups moved toward him. He responded by walking toward her, with his tail still wagging. As the pup approached the big male, she did the play bow. 21 continued to wag his tail and then romped off—a signal that he, too, was willing to play. The pup hesitated, probably because 21 was still a stranger. Then she lay down. He trotted back to her, and as he approached, she jumped up.

Although he was busy with the pup, 21 could tell that 40 was also showing some interest. He had no way of knowing about her aggressive nature, and she was on her best behavior as she tried to impress the handsome newcomer. Moments later, 21 had 40 on one side of him and the playful pup on the other. When 40 did her play bow, 21 happily wagged his tail. Having received a friendly greeting, 21 then moved away from the two Druid wolves, but he stayed close to the pack.

42, the second adult female, was the next Druid to approach. She seemed nervous, almost shy in the presence of this stranger, looking at him, then away, then at him again. He once again wagged his tail to show that he was friendly. 42 slowly came closer and closer until, finally, she was almost touching him.

21 lifted a front paw and gently set it on her shoulder. She responded by laying her chin on his shoulder, and he returned the gesture. After that, 42 gently hit 21 with a paw and did some jump feints, lunging and snapping in the air. She was teasing him ... playing with him. And 21 was enjoying every minute of it. 42 flirted some more by touching her face against his, and then bumping against his big chest. He responded by once

more putting his paw over her shoulder and licking her. Romeo had found his Juliet.

But 40 wasn't about to be left out of the new romance. She ran to them and stood on the opposite side of 21 from 42, as if competing with her sister for 21's attention. But 21 had pretty well made up his mind—and he was definitely more interested in 42.

The five pups now joined the three adults, mobbing 21 as if he were the alpha male returning from a successful hunt. It was their way of letting him know they were very excited about the prospect of him becoming the new adult Druid male—and serving as their adoptive father. And 21 was equally excited about becoming part of this pack.

Wolf 8 had joined the Rose Creek pack after the death of their alpha male, and now his adopted son 21 was joining the Druid pack under the same circumstances. That meant that he would be helping to raise the five pups fathered by Wolf 38 in the same way 8 had raised him and his seven brothers and sisters.

But there were a couple of important differences. Though 21 was more than thirty months old, much older than 8 had been when he joined the Rose Creek pack, he would be faced with challenges 8 had not had to deal with. First of all, the Druids were a family with lots of problems, thanks to the vicious nature of alpha female 40. Because of this, there would always be tension, and at times even danger. Though 21 was bigger and stronger than 40, his instinct to not harm a female in his own pack meant 21 would have to find other ways to keep some sort of peace and harmony within the Druid family.

21's new membership in the Druid pack also meant he had inherited two ongoing feuds. The Druids had killed the Crystal Creek alpha male and injured the alpha female a few years before. The surviving members of that pack, now numbering eight including offspring, controlled a territory just south of where the Druids lived. Because they no longer lived near Crystal Creek, the family was renamed Mollie's pack, in memory of Mollie Beattie, a biologist who had played a major role in bringing wolves back to Yellowstone. If that pack continued to grow, they might decide to try to take back their original territory. This would mean a fight between 21 and the males from the rival Mollie's pack.

There was another possibility as well. The Rose Creek pack that 21 had been a part of until he moved off to join the Druids was not far away either. Which meant the day might come when 21 and his adoptive father and longtime partner, Wolf 8, would be forced into a showdown.

And that day might not be so far off.

I had known 21 for more than two and a half years by the time he joined the Druid pack, and I'd come to realize that he had an easygoing, cooperative personality. Druid female 42 was very much like him, while her sister, Wolf 40, was violent and aggressive. I was sure 21 would be much more compatible with 42 than 40—and my guess turned out to be right. But I also wondered how 8 would feel about 21 becoming a Druid. The original Druid pack had killed 8's father, and Druid male 38 had tried to kill 8. Would 8 think that the son he had adopted and raised had joined what to him was "the enemy"? If that was the case, I worried about what might happen if the two packs met up. By that time I knew that 21 was a bigger, stronger, and faster wolf than 8. ★ RICK

Trouble in the Druid Pack

The spring of 1998 saw a big increase in the size of the Rose Creek pack. Alpha female 9 and one of her daughters had ten pups between them, bringing the number of wolves in the pack to twenty-four—more than double the normal size of a wolf pack.

Meanwhile, their neighbors to the east, the Druids, ended up with only two pups between females 40 and 42. None of 42's pups had survived. It's likely that they were killed by alpha female 40, who had probably wanted to make sure her own pups had enough food and care. She continued to treat the other female wolves in the pack aggressively.

With the three adults (21, 40, and 42), the five yearlings that had been born the previous spring, and the two new pups, there were just ten wolves in the pack. The Druids were less than half the size of the Rose Creek pack, which would be important if the two packs were ever to fight over territory. In the world of wolves, the bigger pack nearly always wins.

But Wolf 21 probably wasn't thinking about the future. He was more concerned with the immediate problems in the pack. 42 was dealing with the loss of her pups and the continual bullying by her sister. 21 was doing all he could to help and comfort the female he had grown so close to. He also didn't really know how to deal with 40. He couldn't bring himself to harm a female wolf, even one as mean and aggressive as 40. And that meant he had to deal with her in other, non-violent ways. Ever since 40 had driven her other sister, 41, out of the family, she'd taken to directing most of her bossiness at 42, probably out of jealousy. But it seemed that the more 40 dominated her sister, the closer 21 and 42 became.

After one particularly harsh incident, 42, injured and frightened, ran to 21 and stood beside him. But 40, still in the grip of one of her rages, clearly wasn't finished with her sister. She approached 42, seemingly intent on continuing the attack. Seeing 21, she stopped in her tracks, unsure of what to do next and uncertain about what might happen if she went after 42 again. 21 did not act aggressively, but nor did he leave 42's side. He simply stood, unmoving and calm, never taking his eyes off 40. He was protecting 42 without becoming the aggressor himself.

It wasn't so different, really, from those times when he was a pup in the acclimation pen and he put himself between the feeding crew and his family. Once again, he was placing himself between a threat and a wolf he wanted to protect. 40 glared at 21 for a few more seconds and then walked away.

Sometimes, to get away from her aggressive sister, 42 would walk away from the pack. And when 21 saw that 42 was off by herself, he would leave the rest of the wolves and join her. Though he was one of the biggest and toughest wolves in Yellowstone, 21 had learned from his adoptive father, Wolf 8, how to be gentle and caring when those qualities were needed.

He also loved to play. Just a couple of days after he'd protected 42 and shown her kindness following her fight with her sister, an opportunity presented itself for the Druids to have some fun—and 21 was all for it.

That morning, female yearling 103 approached 21 and jumped on his back, a surefire sign that she wanted to play. The two immediately began to wrestle. 103 was small, but 21 let her pin him to the ground, pretending to lose, as he often did with the younger wolves. A couple of minutes later, he leaped up and ran off with 103 in pursuit. 21 ran much slower than normal, allowing her to catch up with him. This time she tackled him from behind, got him on the ground again, and then stood over him like a victorious conqueror.

A few hours later 21 was at it again. But this time the games began with the normally grouchy 40. Wolf 21 ran circles around her, then got 40 and the other wolves to chase him. At first 42 stood off to the side, not quite sure what to do. Would 40 attack her if she played too? Eventually, though, she couldn't resist.

21 was having fun, but there was probably more to this play session than just a good time. It looked as if he was trying to act as a peacemaker in his new wolf family. He had included 40 in the play, and that may have caused her to be less aggressive and more cooperative with the other wolves. By the time the session was over, all of the wolves, even 40, had joined in the fun.

That was a long day for me. I had watched the Druids for sixteen hours, but it was worth it! I had seen so much fascinating wolf behavior. I thought about how 8 had adopted and raised 21 and his seven siblings, and how he had played with those pups in the same way I was seeing 21 play with his adopted family. It felt as if 21 was patterning his life more and more after what he had learned from 8— especially when it came to how to be a father. ★ RICK

While 21 was very good at playing with the younger wolves and having fun with his new Druid family, he was equally good at the more serious parts of being the alpha male and an adoptive father. It was only a few days after his play session with 40 and the other Druid wolves that 21 was put to the test. A massive bison—weighing at least a ton (900 kilograms)—happened upon the Druids and immediately charged at them, intent on attacking some of the younger wolves who were having trouble scrambling to safety. As the rest of the pack ran—or tried to run—from the bull, 21 stood his ground. He put all of his 125 pounds (57 kilograms; perhaps as little as one-twentieth of the bison's weight) directly in the path of the gigantic beast.

The bull stopped and glared at 21. The wolf glared back, his low growl the only sound between the two adversaries. After they had stared at each other for a while, 21 decided that he had made his point. He casually turned around and trotted off toward his family. Rather than pursue 21 and the other Druids, the big bison headed off in the opposite direction. Once again, 21 had shown his willingness to put his own life on the line to protect the members of his family.

21 was also very good at the other major responsibility that fell to the alpha male in a pack. He knew that it was his job to provide for his wolf family, and he was willing to do whatever it took to see his family fed. But it wasn't easy, and sometimes his attempts didn't work. As fall rolled in that year, with the leaves changing color and the temperatures slowly dropping, 21 led the family on a hunt. It wasn't long before he and the rest of the Druids surrounded a big bull elk. 21 got behind the elk

and bit into one of his hind legs. At first 21 was able to hang on, but eventually he had to let go to avoid being kicked in the face by the bull's other hind leg. The elk stood his ground, seemingly confident he could handle 21 and the seven other wolves that were surrounding him. The elk even lifted a hind leg and used it to scratch his head, an indicator that he wasn't at all worried about the hunting party. 21 studied the massive elk for a long time and seemed to be weighing the chances of success. Finally, the Druids realized they couldn't handle the bull elk, and, led by 21, they turned and walked off. 21 knew that there would be other hunts, and he was smart enough to save himself and the other wolves in the Druid pack for those days.

Our studies of wolves in Yellowstone suggest that well over 95 percent of wolf hunts end in failure, just like this one did. On average, wolves weigh about 100 pounds (45 kilograms). The animals they hunt in Yellowstone are almost always much larger. Big bull elk can weigh up to 700 pounds (320 kilograms), and bison are even bigger, some weighing in at a ton, so it is a dangerous job to try to kill them. One of Wolf 8's male relatives died in Lamar Valley around that time. I hiked out to check on the cause of death and saw that a bull elk had stabbed him in the chest with his antlers—an example of the danger the wolves could face almost every time they went hunting. In the park, we estimate that 15 percent of our wolves are

killed by prey animals, such as elk and bison, during hunts. Another 50 percent are killed in battles with rival packs over territory. Other causes of death are disease, parasites, accidents, and, when wolves leave the park, hunting and trapping. ★ RICK

Despite 21's peacemaking efforts, 40 continued to be needlessly aggressive to 42 and the three yearling females. One pleasant afternoon, 42 was playing with one of those yearlings when 40 ran over and pinned and bit the younger wolf. It almost seemed as if she was punishing the yearling for playing with 42. When the attack slowed a bit, 42 approached her sister and gently licked her face. That seemed to calm 40 down, and she stopped biting the younger female, but the problem remained. 42 had taken a big risk by intervening, but it demonstrated that she had empathy for the other females her sister mistreated.

More and more, it looked as if 40 wanted to drive out those three yearlings, just as she had driven out her sister 41 and her own mother, Wolf 39. The three yearlings had been born to 41 and 42. Was that why 40 was being so aggressive with them?

Whatever was going on with their aunt didn't stop the yearlings from having fun. On a day when 40 was away from the pack, two yearling females—103 and her bigger sister, 105—wanted to play. The games started with 103 picking up a stick and romping around in front of her sister, daring her to give chase. 105 played along, and after a lengthy chase, the two rested, but only for a little while.

103 did a play bow to get the action started again, then took off with 105 in close pursuit. When the bigger of the two wolves stopped, 103 would throw the stick into the air and catch it. This went on until 103 dropped the stick and allowed 105 to get it, and then hunter became the hunted. When they tired of the chasing game, the sisters wrestled one another, with the larger of the two siblings letting her smaller sister pin her. And on and on it went.

◇ ◇ ◇

Not too far away from Druid territory, the growing Rose Creek pack continued to flourish under 8's leadership. 8 had been with the family for three years now, and had sired nineteen pups. Some were pups born that spring and others were older. 8 was the most successful male wolf in all of Yellowstone when it came to raising pups. What a difference from his early days as an undersized, bullied pup.

For a time, the Rose Creek wolves and the Druid pack, with 21 as the alpha male, seemed to be getting along. There were no fights over food or territory, and there was plenty of food to go around. But that all changed in late 1998. Several young members of the Rose Creek pack strayed into Druid territory—Lamar Valley. One of those young wolves was a female, Wolf 85, who was one of 8's daughters. After wandering around for a time, the young wolves turned and headed back toward their own territory.

But Wolf 85, who was also 21's niece, lagged behind the others and was eventually spotted by the Druids. Led by 40, the Druids chased the young Rose Creek female, caught up with her, and pulled her down. 40, ever the bully, was the lead attacker, repeatedly biting the now helpless Rose Creek wolf. Eventually, the ferocity of the bites proved to be too much, and Wolf 85 died. 21 was there with the rest of the Druids when the attack took place, but he did not participate. Instead, he stood off to one side and looked away. He apparently did not approve of what was happening and refused to be part of it. But he still hadn't figured out how to deal with 40 when she became violent.

21 seemed to live by a rule: he would never do anything to harm a female, even if one bit him. It was an admirable trait, but 40 seemed to be getting more violent as time went by, and the pack needed to find a way to stop her.

Sometimes, 8 would travel through the area where 85 was killed, so it was inevitable that he would one day come across his daughter's remains. And when that happened, 8 would do what wolves do: he'd sniff around the site and pick up the scent of the Druid wolves, including 21. It would be natural for him to conclude that 21 had been involved in killing his daughter. He'd have no way of knowing that the attack had been carried out by 40, and that 21 had not participated in the killing. A confrontation between the two packs was becoming more and more likely. And when it came, it was almost certain that the two alpha males—8 and his adopted son 21—would fight, perhaps to the death.

Let the Games Begin

Every wolf pup and yearling, like every human child, is unique. They each have their own personality traits and quirks. Some are quiet; some are loners; some are endlessly busy. And some are mischievous. Wolf 163, one of the Druid yearlings, definitely fell into that mischievous category. He was always getting into trouble, was curious about everything, and showed almost no fear of humans, which could be a problem in a place like Yellowstone, where there is often a lot of human activity. A wolf that doesn't respect people enough to stay away from them could find himself in danger from cars on the nearby road.

But on one particular spring day in 1999, as the sun was beginning to melt the last of the winter snow, 163 wasn't interested in humans. He just wanted to hang out with his father. First, they fed side by side on a carcass. Then they took a break and began to play. Wolf 21 charged at 163, and then the younger wolf ran at his dad.

21 pretended to be scared and ran off, which led to them taking turns chasing each other back and forth. Then they sparred and wrestled. As he always did when playing with pups and yearlings, 21 held back from using his full strength to keep the match even. As the game went on, the wolves tumbled down a snow-covered hill, rolling over each other several times. When they got to the bottom, they leaped up and 163 again took off after his father. Father and son were having a great time.

Later that spring, new Druid pups were born. When the six-week-old pups—two blacks and four grays—emerged from the den, they played and wrestled with each other and then explored the big wide world. A young adult female, Wolf 106, followed them around, making sure they were safe.

Wolf 163—big brother to these pups—joined the group for some fun. He ran in circles around the pups, played chasing games, and then ran over to a spot where two pups were playing a bit too roughly with a third. The arrival of his older brother gave that pup a chance to get back on its feet, but it didn't seem to mind the roughhousing after all and went right on playing with its siblings.

163 picked up a stick and teased his little brothers and sisters with it, and they chased him around as they tried to steal it. Later, he wrestled with the little pups and let them win—in much the same way 21 had let 163 win when he was a pup.

When the pups got tired, they turned around and headed straight back to the den, showing off what was already a good sense of direction.

I tried to keep track of all the different types of games the Druid and Rose Creek pups played. A favorite could be called the "stealing game." One pup would pick up a bone. Another pup would come over, grab the bone, and run off with it. The first pup would then give chase. Another game involved a pup sneaking up behind a sibling and pulling its tail. And still another favorite was "king of the mountain," where one would get up on a rock or log and try to prevent the other pups from climbing up. ★ RICK

◇ ◇ ◇

Summer soon arrived, and with it, a different kind of danger to the young wolves. While wandering onto the road or getting too close to humans was always a concern, bears were an equally serious threat. Bears often compete with wolves for the same food sources. And that summer, black bears were proving to be a problem for the Druids, often coming into the den area. One morning, 42 led her six pups out of the den area. A few minutes later, she and five of the pups had disappeared into a stand of trees. But one small black pup was having trouble keeping up, which left him alone out in the open. And that's exactly when a mother black bear with two cubs happened along. 42 must have realized one pup was missing, for she soon ran back out of the trees. When she saw the bear family, she rushed over to the slow pup and walked side by side with it, leading it away from the bears. As they traveled, she bent and licked the pup to encourage it to keep going. By keeping the little wolf's spirits up, she was able to save it from the lurking danger.

By July, the six Druid pups were starting to get interested in hunting. In fact, they were teaching themselves the first things they would need to know in order to be successful adult hunters. There was a marsh not far from the den, and the pups discovered that small mouselike animals called voles lived there. All six pups were fascinated by the voles and, after studying the little marsh rodents for a while, graduated to catching and eating them. A pup would catch a vole, let it go, catch it again, and then repeat the process a few more times. With 21 lying nearby and watching his offspring, all six pups got better and better at catching the voles. It was a small but important step in building their hunting skills.

Later that month the Druids were on the move. Seven adults and six pups headed south in single file from the den to the family's "rendezvous site"—a new home base where the pups could be left safely on their own while the adult wolves went out on hunts. Wolf pups like to explore, so they quickly and eagerly took to their new quarters. 21 and 42 watched over the pups as they got used to their surroundings. During one of the frequent walks the parents and pups took, a young wolf passed 21 and confidently led the group. That pup was a natural-born leader. The pups' exploration of the surrounding terrain paid dividends when they discovered another marsh with a large population of voles. And once again, the hunt was on.

While black bears were an occasional problem at the den location, the rendezvous site came with an even bigger threat: grizzlies. That August, a mother grizzly and her three cubs strolled into the area. 21 immediately charged at the sow, biting her on the rear end to get her to leave. It was a tactic he had perfected. 21 was faster and more agile than the grizzlies, so he could get away with harassing them into leaving. And though the grizzly mother didn't really seem eager to leave, she finally took the hint and decided to give her backside a break. With a final snort in 21's direction, she led her cubs into the trees and away.

◇ ◇ ◇

That year, 1999, was another tough year for 42. She once again had no surviving pups, and it was almost a certainty that her sister, Wolf 40, had gone into the den when 42 was away and killed the pups. 40's constant bullying, particularly of 42, and her extreme behavior—the killing of 42's pups—were doing great harm to the

Druid pack. Those pups had been fathered by 21, so it was a terrible loss for him as well.

42 was the complete opposite of her sister in temperament. She treated the younger adult females, 103, 105, and 106, with kindness, while 40 was as aggressive with them as she was with most of the wolves in the family. Those females had good reason to dislike and distrust 40, and they much preferred spending time with 42.

One summer day, a couple of the yearlings ran past 40 in a race to greet 42, who they liked to play with. Not surprisingly, 40 immediately ran toward 42 and displayed the dominant, aggressive posture she often adopted around her sister. 42 dropped to the ground and rolled onto her back. 40 snapped at her and moved off. But when 42 got back up into a crouch, 40 snapped at her again. For a second time, 42 rolled onto her back. This time she also licked 40's face, trying to appease her and demonstrate subordinate status. This was 40 at her jealous worst. It seemed like she was angry that her sister was more popular with the younger wolves.

Nearby, 21 had been watching, and he decided to do something to relieve the tension. He approached 40 and started to play. The young wolves joined in and a rollicking game of chasing followed, with 40 and 21 taking turns both at chasing and at being chased. For a long time 42 stood apart from the others. As she had during other play sessions, she seemed worried about what would happen if she joined in. Eventually, she began to play too, although she stuck mostly to the yearlings. The pack was back to normal and peace had been restored, thanks to the actions of 21. Though he was the biggest and toughest of all the wolves, he had shown again and again that he was willing to do whatever it took to maintain harmony in the family, even if that meant playing the part of class clown.

42 continued to have a special relationship with 21. When 21 was traveling with the pack, he would look back often to check on her, as if making sure she was safe and keeping up. And their affection was obvious when they played together. One day, 21 approached 42 with his head low, acting like he was a young wolf approaching the pack's alpha female. He went into a crouch and rolled on his back. 42 stood over him with a raised tail, but it was wagging in a friendly manner. Then 21 lifted his head and licked her face in the way a low-ranking wolf would greet a higher-ranking one. It looked as if he was letting his mate pretend that she was an alpha female.

◇ ◇ ◇

The Rose Creek pack continued to be a force in that part of Yellowstone. Earlier that year, as spring brought warmer temperatures and gentle winds to the park,

8 decided to take advantage of a particularly pleasant day to take the family on a hunt. He set off with four young adult pups, and it wasn't long before they came across a cow elk. All five wolves took off after the elk, but soon the four younger wolves were far ahead of their father. 8 was struggling hard to keep up, something he had seldom had to do in his entire life. The four younger wolves reached the cow elk and fought with her, but they were losing the battle. 8 finally caught up to the scene of the struggle and quickly put his leadership and experience to good use. The tide turned almost immediately, and the wolves were at last able to bring the elk down and finish the kill. Had 8 not been there, the young wolves would never have gotten the job done. Though 8 was getting older, he was still a great warrior among the wolves of Yellowstone, able to pull his weight and more.

In 2000, several of us who had observed the Yellowstone wolves over the years tried to figure out how many pups 8 had fathered since he joined the Rose Creek pack in late 1995. It worked out to a total of just over fifty. In addition, he had also raised 21 and the other seven pups that had lost their biological father. That was very impressive for a wolf who, when he was young, had looked like he would never amount to anything. ★ RICK

Time Marches On

The temperature that day in December 1999 was 15 degrees Fahrenheit (about minus 10 degrees Celsius), and 8 was up early and ready to lead his family on a hunt in the Slough Creek area. They hadn't gone far when 8 spotted a young elk and gave chase. The elk ran into the creek and stood in water that was almost 3 feet (close to 1 meter) deep. The Rose Creek wolves arrived at the edge of the creek and stared at the elk. Though the water wasn't frozen, it was very cold, and 8 and the other wolves knew that. But 8 didn't hesitate. He charged into the water after the elk.

None of the other wolves joined their father, so at first it was just 8—who weighed less than 100 pounds (45 kilograms)—battling it out with an elk that probably weighed three times that much. One wolf, one elk, freezing water.

The elk charged at 8, then reared up and tried to stomp him with its front hooves. 8 dodged that blow, and also a second attempted stomping. The elk tried again, and this time it hit 8 on the top of his head with its rock-hard hooves.

. But as the elk struck 8, it lost its balance and fell into the water. 8 saw his chance. He put aside the pain of the kick and charged the elk again. He chased it through the creek as the other wolves remained on shore watching, too afraid of getting hurt to join in the battle.

The fight continued with first 8 and then the enraged elk charging at one another. But 8 was tiring and growing weaker. He'd been in the frigid water for a long time. The elk once again reared up on its hind legs. This time, it came down with both front hooves on 8's back, driving him underwater. If the elk could keep him down there long enough, 8 would drown. But somehow the wolf broke free and struggled to the surface.

8 was badly injured and dazed, and it didn't look like he'd be able to continue or even defend himself. But he needed to feed his family, and he wasn't about to give up.

It was at that moment that he finally got some help. One of his young sons or daughters jumped into the creek, and together the two wolves charged the elk again. It kicked the younger wolf, forcing it underwater, but the yearling resurfaced and continued to fight.

Now the elk too was tiring. 8 jumped up out of the water and grabbed its throat. The younger wolf helped out by biting into a hind leg. The elk kicked back with its other hind leg, hitting the yearling in the head and knocking it off. Ignoring the pain, the young wolf bit into that leg again. Then it let go, ran through the water to 8, and both wolves worked together to finish off the elk and pull it up on the ice.

The battle was over, but the wolves' triumph came at a steep cost. 8 was badly hurt. At almost six years old, 8 had already lived a year longer than the average wolf in Yellowstone. He was an old wolf now, and while he'd won this match—and many other battles with much bigger opponents—those encounters had taken a heavy toll on his body.

During my early years in Yellowstone I worked from the spring through late fall. But in 1999 my assignment changed; now I would be working year-round. That meant I was about to experience my first winter in the park. I had previously been stationed in desert national parks such as Death Valley during the winters, and I was worried that I would find it hard to deal with the very cold temperatures in Yellowstone.

I lived in the small town of Silver Gate, Montana, located a mile (about 1.5 kilometers) outside of the northeast entrance to the park. The town was 7,390 feet (2,250 meters) above sea level, meaning the winter temperatures would be especially frigid. During that season, there were only seven of us in the town.

One benefit of wintertime in Yellowstone would be the shorter days. In the summer I got up at 3:15 a.m. so I would

have time to get ready and be out in the park looking for wolves as soon as there was enough light to see (around 5 a.m.). But in winter, I'd be able to sleep in much longer due to the later sunrise. I figured I'd be able to "sleep in" until about 5:30 a.m. ★ RICK

◇ ◇ ◇

A few weeks later on a bitterly cold Christmas morning, 8 and his family were gathered at Slough Creek. Not far away was an elk carcass that still had a lot of meat on it. 8 and the other wolves had fed and were now full and resting. While the wolves slept and relaxed after their hunt, several coyotes snuck up to the carcass, intent on stealing some food. 8 raised his head, looked toward the elk carcass and spotted the coyotes. He wasn't about to allow the smaller animals to steal his family's precious meat. He leaped up, and with two of the young wolves alongside, raced toward the carcass to chase the thieves away.

The snow was deep in that area. The wolves had tramped it down to form a kind of pit around the elk. The three wolves surrounded a young coyote pup, the only one that hadn't run off to escape the attack. The wolves were much bigger than the young coyote and quickly got it down in the snow, where they began to bite it at will. It wouldn't be long before the coyote was dead.

8 had good reason to want to kill that coyote. Wolves and coyotes are natural enemies. All wolves have a grudge against the smaller, wily animals, mostly because coyotes will steal wolves' food every chance they get, just as this pack had wanted to do. And now here was one of the culprits, caught, defenseless, and at the mercy of 8 and the other two wolves.

A raven landed nearby, no doubt anticipating a meal of coyote meat. But after a short time, 8 ended his attack on the intruder. Because he was the leader, the other two wolves also stopped biting the helpless and hapless coyote. 8 then led the other wolves away from the site and back to the rest of the pack, where the three food protectors bedded down once again.

Though 8 knew that the coyote was an adversary, he had decided to give it a break. After a few minutes the coyote raised its head, looked around, and saw that the wolves were gone. It got to its feet, shook itself, and ran off to join the rest of its pack. Just as when 8 had fought and defeated 38 some years before in almost the same area, he saw no reason to kill the young coyote.

◇ ◇ ◇

Meanwhile, that same Christmas Day, the Druid wolves were on familiar ground in Lamar Valley. December's deep snow made travel for the wolves difficult. They traveled to the west for a while, then stopped to rest.

21 usually led the pack, which meant that he did the exhausting work of breaking a trail in the thick snow. But this born leader was also smart. If he came across a trail in the snow made by bison or elk, he would use it to conserve his energy and that of the other wolves in the pack. Due to 21's work, 42 and the other Druids had a much easier time as they traveled behind him on days like this.

21 and 42 were soon at play. 21 rolled on his back under her, once again behaving like a low-ranking wolf. Two of the younger wolves saw what was going on, ran over, and also stood over 21. Soon he jumped up and romped off with a tucked tail as a pup chased him. He ran back to 42, circled around her, and then fell over— like a comedian trying to get a laugh from an audience. If wolves could laugh, there would be no one better than 21 at making it happen. The young Druids were having fun that day, and so was their father.

There was no doubt that 21 was the toughest wolf in all of Yellowstone, and he could use that toughness when he needed to. But when he was with 42 and the younger wolves, he loved nothing better than to play.

And while most of that play was just about having fun, 21 seemed to be aware that playing with 42 was a little different. Their play sessions likely gave her a welcome break from the abuse 40 inflicted on her. Whatever else was going on in 42's life, she at least had these happy moments of playtime with 21.

I had often heard the Druid and Rose Creek wolves howling at each other. Each time that happened I was worried, for I knew that sooner or later the neighboring packs would meet up. The two primary jobs of alpha male wolves are to feed and protect their families. I had seen 8 fight and defeat Wolf 38 when the earlier version of the Druids charged at the Rose Creek wolves. 21 was equally dedicated to protecting his pack, and over his long life I had never seen him lose a fight with another male wolf. 8 was now an old wolf who was suffering from many injuries, while 21 was younger and very strong. To me, he seemed invincible. I had seen him fight six rival wolves at once and win that battle. I dreaded the possibility of a confrontation between these two packs. ★ RICK

10

The Battle

It was a cool, cloudy, unpleasant day in early 2000, almost exactly five years after wolves had been reintroduced to Yellowstone National Park. The Rose Creek wolves were in the west end of Lamar Valley—Druid territory. This was the third day in a row that the Rose Creek pack had been in the area normally occupied by the Druids, and once again they were howling. But unlike earlier howling contests between the two packs, this time there were no answering howls. Instead, the Druids were on the march, heading toward the Rose Creek pack. In the lead for the Druids was 40. The aggressive, often vicious female appeared to have just one thing on her mind: she was going to lead an attack on the rival pack—the Rose Creek wolves.

The Druids stopped and had a big group howl. They were loudly proclaiming their right to this territory. The Rose Creek wolves howled back. It sounded like they were challenging the Druids to a fight. Bad blood had been simmering between the two packs ever since 40 had killed the young Rose Creek female, and now it looked like the two families were finally going to fight.

The Druids stopped howling and took off at top speed, heading directly for the Rose Creek wolves. They raced toward the other pack, running up a ridge to reach their opponents. Now 21 was out in front, his normal position when he felt his pack was in danger. He looked deadly serious and was clearly at the peak of his strength and fighting ability.

From the opposite direction, also running at top speed, the Rose Creek pack raced toward the Druids with 8 in the lead. Just like 21, he was dedicated to protecting his family. But there was a difference—actually a few differences. 8 was older than his adopted son, and he had suffered many injuries over the years. It was a mismatch, with 8 having almost no chance of defeating the bigger and stronger 21, and yet he continued his charge straight at the younger wolf. His family was under threat, and 8 would fight, and die if needed, to protect them.

But it was a fight that didn't have to happen. It had been the vicious Wolf 40, not 21, who had killed the young Rose Creek female, and she was the real cause of the tension between the packs. Nevertheless, 8 and 21 shared one priority on this day: protect their family—even if this meant facing off against each other.

There was one important factor that might save the day. Neither of the two warriors who were about to do battle had killed their defeated enemies. 8 had allowed 38 to live and go back to his family. 21 had seen that incident, and it appeared that he'd taken the lesson to heart. In all his fights and all of his victories, 21 had not once killed an opponent. But there was a problem. 40, a known wolf killer, was right behind 21. If the two alpha males fought and 21 pinned 8, it would be only a matter of seconds before 40 would join in with a savage attack. It had happened before with the young Rose Creek female, and there was no reason to think it wouldn't happen again. It was a virtual certainty that if 8 lost the fight with his adopted son, 40 would not let him survive.

The two packs were closing fast, and the two alpha males, each out in front of his pack, were about to collide. The battle was about to begin.

Then, at the last possible second, the unthinkable happened. 21 veered slightly away from 8, shot past him and the rest of his pack, and then continued to run. The other Druids were stunned and confused. Was their leader afraid of the enemy Rose Creek pack? If so, maybe they should be as well. They all followed 21's example and ran past 8 and the other Rose Creek wolves.

It's likely that even 8 wasn't sure what had just happened. But he hesitated for only a few seconds before he turned and chased after 21. The rest of his pack followed him. And then things quickly became chaotic. Both packs began to split up, with wolves chasing other wolves, but there wasn't any real fighting. At one point, four Rose Creek wolves pursued 21, but he easily outran them. What could have been a deadly battle had turned into a chasing game, and the battlefield had become an unexpected playground. It was somewhat like what had happened on that first day when 8 had met 21 and the other pups and they all played chasing games. Soon the Rose Creek wolves got together up high on the ridge, while all the Druids gathered downhill from them. As the Druids drifted off, the wolves in 8's group lay down, exhausted from all the running. The war that had never really happened was over. No wolves died or were even injured that day.

The following morning, the Druids were in the east end of Lamar Valley and the Rose Creek wolves had returned to Slough Creek, to the west. The crisis appeared to be over. And it was all because 21 refused to fight 8, the wolf that had adopted and raised him.

An Ending

With spring came the birth of new pups. Both 40 and 42 had litters that had been fathered by 21. To avoid a repeat of 40 killing her pups, 42 denned several miles west of 40's den site. Three younger females also had litters that spring, and two of them were based at 42's den.

For a while after the birth of the pups, there was relative peace in Lamar Valley. Mothers cared for their newborns while adult males hunted and brought back food for the families. Both 40's and 42's dens were safe havens for the mothers and pups. But the time of tranquility came to an end late one gentle spring day.

40 left her pups, trotted west, and disappeared into the trees where her sister was denning. Once again, it seemed, she was intent on killing 42's pups. But this time, there was a difference. For the first time in her life, 42 was ready to stand up to her sister and protect her pups.

The problem for 42 was that 40 was not only more aggressive and mean, but also stronger and a better fighter. Though her act of defiance was brave, 42 was quickly overpowered. It seemed as if the fight would be short, and whether 40 decided to let 42 live or not, there was no doubt that when it was over she would kill her sister's pups.

But then everything changed, and in a way 40 could never have expected. Over the years, she'd picked on all of the female wolves in the pack, not just her sister. And now two of those young females—Wolves 103 and 105, who had litters of their own at that site—came to the aid of their aunt 42, who had always treated them well.

Suddenly the fight wasn't just 40 against 42. It was 40 against three of her previous victims. As tough as 40 was, she was no match for three mothers who were determined to protect their pups, and who had had enough of being bullied. 42 and her new allies soon had 40 on the ground, and they did to her what she done so many times to so many others.

Defeated and badly injured, 40 dragged herself away from the scene of the fight, eventually taking shelter in a culvert. She was covered with blood and lying in freezing-cold water. That is where Rick found her. She was alive, but there were bite marks on her belly and rear end and a gaping wound on the back of her neck. As Rick and law enforcement officer Mike Ross knelt next to her, they could see she was in shock.

The decision about whether or not to intervene was an easy one. This was a mother with newborn pups. If she died, there was a good chance that her pups would starve to death. And so, they would try to save her. Carefully wrapping and taping her jaws and paws to prevent her doing harm to them or herself, the two men bundled 40 inside a blanket and gently eased her into the back seat of their pickup truck. They made a stop at the Lamar Ranger Station, where Mike lived. Rick stayed with 40 while Mike ran inside and filled several jugs with hot water. He also called a veterinarian for advice on what they could do to save 40.

The two men set the jugs around 40's body and turned on the truck's heater in an attempt to raise her extremely low body temperature, the result of her lying for a long time in the culvert's frigid water. They had done all they could for the Druid's alpha female, but their efforts to save 40 were not successful. She died from blood loss and shock.

That meant there was another problem that would have to be dealt with—and quickly. What would happen to 40's newborn pups, who now had no mother to feed and care for them? There were other questions that needed answers as well. Had 40 succeeded in killing any of 42's pups before she was attacked? And if so, would 42 or any of the other females allow 40's pups to nurse and receive the nourishment they would need to survive?

With 40 gone from the den, 21 was doing his best to care for their pups. But at this stage of their lives, the pups relied on their mother's milk to keep them alive. 21, the great hunter, fighter, and father, could do nothing to help his offspring. The only way for 40's pups to survive was for another nursing mother to allow them to drink.

Meanwhile, 42 returned to her den and soon emerged with six pups. That meant 40 had not succeeded in killing any of 42's pups before the attack that led to her death.

Two days later, 21 brought 42 to 40's den to help with the hungry pups, but he had no way of knowing how she would respond. Although 40 hadn't killed any of 42's pups this year, she had certainly done so in the past. Would 42 now seek revenge and kill her vicious sister's pups?

42 disappeared into 40's den. She was inside for a long time before she finally came out and returned to her own den. Over the next few days, 42 and one of the younger females carried puppies in their mouths to the den housing 40's pups. To get there, the wolves had to swim across a creek with the pups held high to keep them from drowning. Eventually, 42 and the three younger Druid mothers had moved all of their pups to the main den. But 40's pups still hadn't been spotted, and the mystery remained: Were 40's pups alive and in

that den, being fed by the other females? Or had they met a different fate?

Some weeks later, those questions were answered at last. 21 had just chased off a grizzly that had tried to take over a carcass. When he returned to the main den he received the ritual greeting from the pups, fifteen in all. But soon more pups joined the happy mob. There were thirteen blacks and eight grays, twenty-one pups all together. Wolf litters average four to five pups, which implied there were five litters at the den—and one of them had to be 40's. 42 and the other young wolf mothers had been feeding them, along with their own.

Caring for that number of pups took tremendous organization and leadership from 42, who graduated to the role of alpha female after 40's death. And it also took cooperation and a willingness from all the wolves to work together, something that had been missing from the Druid pack when 40 was alive and running things. The adult females came together to care for the large band of pups, while the adult males made foray after foray into the woods to track and kill the prey that would be essential for feeding the large brood and their mothers. While it would continue to be a difficult and challenging task for all of the Druids to manage this very large family, the peace and harmony that had triumphed over the violence of 40's leadership were a good start. A very good start indeed.

12

Farewell

The late spring sun was warming the woods of Yellowstone National Park. 18, a Rose Creek female, had recently given birth to pups, and 8 decided to go off on a hunt to bring back meat to the young wolves. He was by himself and in no hurry as he patrolled the woodlands he knew so well.

After searching the deep forest for elk, he lay down for a while and let the sun's soothing rays work their healing magic on a body that had taken tremendous punishment over the years. Broken teeth, injuries all over his body, a damaged jaw, and a head that had sustained numerous kicks from the powerful elk—the toll had reached the point that 8 was clearly nearing the end of his remarkable life.

But on this day, 8 didn't let any of that slow him down. After resting for a few minutes, he got back to his feet and resumed his search for food. It wasn't long before he spotted a big cow elk. The elk saw 8 at almost exactly the same time and immediately ran into a nearby stream. 8 didn't hesitate. As he had done many times before, he took to the water and attacked the big female.

She fought back and kicked him off, once, then twice. 8 shook off the hard kicks and resumed his attack, finally managing to get his powerful jaws on one of the elk's hind legs. She kicked at him again and again. And finally, she connected, the full power of her leg and that lethal hoof striking 8's head with deadly force.

His grip loosened and the great alpha wolf fell into the water, stunned by the repeated kicks. He struggled, knowing he had to get to shore or drown. But for the first time in his life 8 didn't have the strength to continue. The body that had taken so much punishment simply gave out. The small gray wolf that had defied the odds so many times had nothing left. He tried one last time for the shore, but it was no use. He had fought his last fight. Knowing he was not going to survive, 8 relaxed his body and prepared to die. The current carried his body downstream, where it would later be found by Yellowstone's wolf biologists.

8 died as he had lived, serving his family. Dying in combat was a noble, honorable end to an extraordinary life. As the water of the creek flowed over and around his body, was 8 able to look back at his life and feel

contented? It's unlikely, maybe, but a nice thought to have. If ever a wolf had reason to be proud of what he was and what he had done, it was the little gray wolf that had begun life as the runt victim of his bullying brothers and had grown up to be one of the greatest wolves who ever lived in Yellowstone National Park.

We found out later how badly 8 had been hurt during the fights he'd had with other wolves and a number of elk. Several of his teeth had been broken off by kicks to the head, and there were other serious injuries as well. After his death, an expert examined his skeleton and made a list of those injuries, especially the ones to his head. She summed up her findings by saying: "I do not understand how an animal could have lived through this." We suspect that all those blows to the head also damaged 8's brain. In fact, he may have had the same type of brain injuries that many professional football players have. Those men all wear helmets, while 8 had nothing to protect his head.

The only way I can understand how 8 lived through it all is to say that he was the toughest animal I have ever known. He was willing to pay any cost to feed and protect his family. But as I watched 8 in his older years, I knew that all the wear and tear on his body was rapidly weakening him. He no longer had the strength and stamina that he'd had as a young wolf.

As the end drew nearer for 8, I tried to prepare myself for the death I knew was inevitable. That was not easy. I have said elsewhere in this book that I was drawn to the study of wolves in part by their similarity to humans in the way they care for their families and interact with other wolves in play, in love, and even in combat. 8 was much more to me than a specimen to observe and study. He was not a companion the way a family dog is to many of us; in fact, we did not normally interfere with the natural progression of the wolves' lives. And yet, he was as special to me as any family pet could ever be. I had spent thousands of hours watching him live his life. I admired his heroism, laughed at his playfulness, feared at times for his safety, and, most of all, I liked him. Now, many years later, I still think about him and marvel at the amazing life of the wolf I had come to know so well—Wolf 8. ★ RICK

Afterword
We Are All Related

JOHN POTTER

When I was young, I heard the same horror stories about Wolves that many of you probably heard. Do you remember the Wolf that surprises Little Red Riding Hood at her grandmother's cottage, or the one that torments the Three Little Pigs? So many stories of the "Big Bad Wolf." And all that huffing and puffing and "My, what big teeth you have!"

I probably should've been terrified of Wolves, but I never was. I actually thought the Three Little Pigs deserved to have their houses blown down. They shouldn't have built them on Wolf's native homeland in the first place!

I probably should've had nightmares about Wolves, but I never did. In my dreams, I was talking with them, running and playing with them, hunting with them, howling with them. In my dreams, their tracks were like prayers left for me to step in—not step *on*.

I think I actually told my mother once that I was part Wolf.

I loved to draw when I was young (and I still do—as you can see from the illustrations of Wolf 8 and others in this book). At some point, I began drawing Wolves based on the ones I saw in my dreams. My mom gave me sketchbooks and pencils, but I did not just sit still and draw quietly at the kitchen table. I took my sketchbooks out into the hills and forests, and along the lakes near my home, and I drew everything and anything that would sit still long enough for me to draw it. Drawing helped me make sense of the world. Drawing in Nature made me fall in love with the world.

As I grew older, my passion for knowing, understanding, and expressing the beauty of the Natural World—and of Wolves in particular—took hold of my heart. The more I learned about our Indigenous relationship with the Wild and with Wildlife, the more I wanted to be a Wolf when I grew up!

But then, really, aren't we all Wolves?

I've been told that "primitive" human hunters would "shadow" Wolf packs that were out hunting. In my imagination, I can see Wolves shadowing human hunters as their hunting prowess evolved. In my imagination, I can believe that, as our ancient relationship matured, we and Wolves hunted cooperatively. (Those Wolves eventually became our "dogs.") In my imagination, I see Wolves and early humans feeding at the same kills, howling in celebration together, feeding our growing families, sharing stories and wisdom—moving with a common understanding of, and a reverence for, what it means to walk on this good Earth in balance.

In one way or another, Wolves fed us—even if only by example. We humans would not be here today if not for Wolves, and if not for our earliest observations of them—learning *from* them, not just about them. And I think it's time that we acknowledge that, and return the favor by feeding *them*. Feed them by inviting them back to the home and table of our hearts and minds. Feed them with respect and decency, and by honoring their right to be here with us on these lands and on this good Earth. This is the "food" they need now, from us.

This is why my brother and I, at the invitation of Yellowstone National Park, came to perform welcoming and adoption Ceremonies for the Wolves during both reintroduction phases, in 1995 and 1996. It was our way of giving back. Our way of feeding them.

I'd like to offer a little bit of one of our Ojibwe origin stories—one that's told and shared widely in the Anishinaabe world:

> As Original Man walked the Earth (which we think of as our Original Mother), he came to know, understand, and communicate with all living Creation. And as he became a Relative of all, he noticed that the animals came in pairs, and that they raised families. But he was alone.

He decided to ask Creator about the situation. "What's up with this?" he said. "Why am I alone, with no one else who looks like me?"

"Fine, then," Creator answered. "I will send someone for you to hang out with, someone who can be your best friend."

And so, Creator sent Maa'iingan—Wolf.

"You are to be brother to one another, from here on out," Creator said.

Side by side, Wolf and Original Man walked the entire Earth together, growing closer to each other with each passing day. They became brothers with all living things, and gave names to all that is.

After much time had passed, Creator told them it was time to part, and that each should go their own way. But even though they would now walk separately, they would still be connected.

"Whatever happens to one of you will happen to the other as well," Creator told them. "Know that you will both be feared and misunderstood by another people yet to come."

Over time, we as Native People have seen this to be true. Over time, we and Wolves came to be much alike. We have both had our lands taken from us, and occupied. We have both been hunted down, and pushed close to vanishing altogether.

But over time, we as *humans* are also beginning to awaken to, and understand, the Native concept we call

Gakina Awiiya—"We Are All Related." Science is even beginning to catch up to us in its understanding of the interconnectedness—the interdependency—of all life on this planet.

We all "relate to" and feed each other. What happens to one species happens to, and has an effect on, *all.*

I hope that we find it in our collective heart and consciousness to include Wolves at the table as we "feed on" these new—and old—understandings. I hope that we can quit huffing and puffing and trying to blow everything down, and instead let ourselves run and play and howl together in celebration and wonder of what we share with all that is still wild.

I hope that, with the help of books like this one, we leave prayers in our tracks for our great-grandchildren to step in, not step on.

Acknowledgments

I would like to thank the team at Greystone Books for bringing my writing about the wolves of Yellowstone to a new audience, and my editor Linda Pruessen for doing an excellent job on pulling this book together. I had a great time working with her and with my co-writer David A. Poulsen, whose storytelling skills made the book much better than what I could have done on my own. A special thanks to my friend John Potter for his beautiful artwork and essay on the relationship between Native and Indigenous people and wolves. ★ RICK

Special thanks to Greystone Books for putting their faith in me to tackle this project and for their endless support during its completion; to Rick McIntyre, who has made it his life's work to study and write about wolves and who was endlessly patient as we took his creations and together made new stories for new audiences; and to Linda Pruessen, first for recommending me for this book and then for her wisdom and guidance as she once again worked her editing magic to make it so much better. ★ DAVID

About the Authors

RICK MCINTYRE has spent more time observing and documenting wolves in the wild than any other person. A retired National Park Service ranger, Rick has watched wolves in America's national parks for more than forty-four years, twenty-eight of those in Yellowstone, where he has accumulated over 100,000 wolf sightings, worked on the Yellowstone Wolf Reintroduction Project, and educated the public about the park's wolves, including by writing several books for adult readers (*The Rise of Wolf 8*, *The Reign of Wolf 21*, *The Redemption of Wolf 302*, and *The Alpha Female Wolf*). He lives in Silver Gate, Montana. To learn more about him and his books, visit rickmcintyrebooks.com.

DAVID A. POULSEN is the author of twenty-eight books, many of them for middle readers. His young adult novel *Numbers* was selected for the Sakura Medal (awarded by English-speaking high school students in Japan to their favorite novel of the year). His teen/young adult novel *And Then the Sky Exploded* was a nominee for the 2018 Ontario Library Association's Red

Maple Award. He divides his time between Saskatoon, Saskatchewan; Maricopa, Arizona; and Claresholm, Alberta. To learn more about David and his work, visit davidapoulsenauthor.com.